W9-BUF-132

PRAISE FOR ASHLEY CRAFT'S
The Unofficial Universal Theme Parks Cookbook

"Ashley has knocked it out of the (theme) park again! *The Unofficial Universal Theme Parks Cookbook* is jam-packed with delicious, easy-to-follow recipes for chefs at every skill level. It's a must-have for every Universal Studios fan!"

—**Kelly Short**, *Navigating Joyful Challenges*

"WOW! *The Unofficial Universal Theme Parks Cookbook* opens up with short descriptions of each Universal land, and how the food/drinks available in those lands tie in with the stories surrounding them. It caused us not only to make a mental note to book a trip to the Parks soon—but in the short term, it made us SO excited to jump in and try out some of our favorite recipes. Ashley's creative narrative takes this to a whimsical yet informative level, and her recipes are straightforward and easy to follow (even for an inexperienced cook such as myself!). Re-creating food or drinks you know and love can be a daunting task, but *The Unofficial Universal Theme Parks Cookbook* makes it a breeze. We love being able to experience the Parks at home via some of our favorite dishes out of Ashley's cookbook!"

—**Kalyn Liesmann**, *Must Have Magic*

"Whether you're a fan of the Universal Theme Parks or just their fantastic properties—from Harry Potter to Minions, The Simpsons to Dr. Seuss—this cookbook is the most delicious way to bring Universal magic into your home. No family movie night, character-inspired play, or themed birthday party is complete without Ashley's Universal-inspired recipes—which means no family kitchen is complete without this book. From Korean Corn Dogs to No Melt Ice Cream (the perfect Happy Potter party treat), this book is full of recipes that not only bring major food joy but feed your family well too. And that's as magical as it gets!"

—**Stacie Billis**, *Didn't I Just Feed You*

"I love all the included backstory about the Parks. The food choices are so good, I didn't even know some of them existed! It makes me want to go back to Universal and try them all. I also love The Universal Parks Cook's Essentials chapter—so helpful!"

—**Deana Romano**, *Deana Style*

"This book brings the magic of Universal home to you. Enjoying these delicious recipes makes you feel like you're at the Parks without leaving the comfort of your home. We can't wait to host a party for our friends and surprise them with their favorite Park foods and drinks."

—**Kari and Amanda**, *Sunshine Seekers*

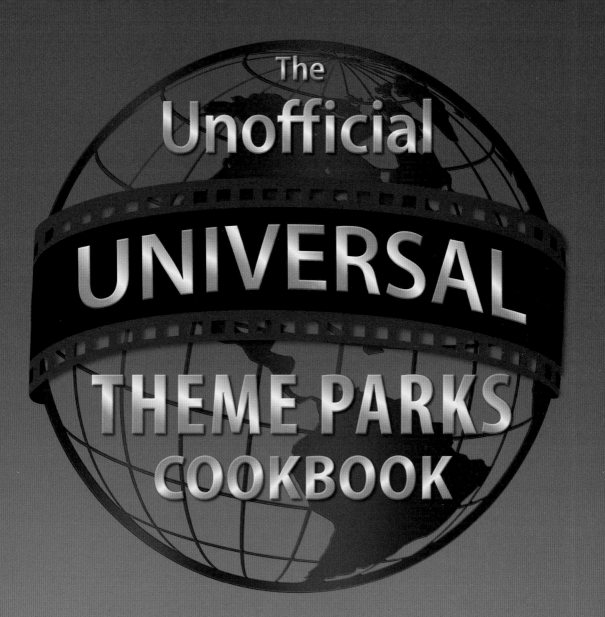

The Unofficial

UNIVERSAL

THEME PARKS
COOKBOOK

FROM MOOSE JUICE TO
CHICKEN AND WAFFLE SANDWICHES,
75+ DELICIOUS UNIVERSAL-INSPIRED RECIPES

ASHLEY CRAFT
Author of the *USA TODAY* Bestselling *The Unofficial Disney Parks Cookbook*

ADAMS MEDIA
NEW YORK   LONDON   TORONTO   SYDNEY   NEW DELHI

Adams Media
An Imprint of Simon & Schuster, Inc.
100 Technology Center Drive
Stoughton, Massachusetts 02072

Copyright © 2022 by Ashley Craft.

All rights reserved, including the right to reproduce this book or portions thereof in any form whatsoever. For information address Adams Media Subsidiary Rights Department, 1230 Avenue of the Americas, New York, NY 10020.

First Adams Media hardcover edition October 2022

ADAMS MEDIA and colophon are trademarks of Simon & Schuster.

For information about special discounts for bulk purchases, please contact Simon & Schuster Special Sales at 1-866-506-1949 or business@simonandschuster.com.

The Simon & Schuster Speakers Bureau can bring authors to your live event. For more information or to book an event contact the Simon & Schuster Speakers Bureau at 1-866-248-3049 or visit our website at www.simonspeakers.com.

Interior design by Sylvia McArdle
Interior photographs by Harper Point Photography
Photography chefs: Christine Tarango and Abraham Lemus
Interior illustrations by Alaya Howard
Maps by Russell Tate
Interior images © 123RF

Manufactured in the United States of America

10 9 8 7 6 5 4 3 2 1

Library of Congress Cataloging-in-Publication Data has been applied for.

ISBN 978-1-5072-1821-1
ISBN 978-1-5072-1822-8 (ebook)

Many of the designations used in this book, including but not limited to place names and character names, are the registered trademarks of NBCUniversal Media LLC, its affiliates, or various third parties. Where those designations appear in the book and the publisher is aware of the trademark status, the designations have been printed with initial capital letters.

Always follow safety and commonsense cooking protocols while using kitchen utensils, operating ovens and stoves, and handling uncooked food. If children are assisting in the preparation of any recipe, they should always be supervised by an adult.

DEDICATION

For my siblings, Jamie, Brett, and Kelly,
for being my assistants on research trips!

CONTENTS

ACKNOWLEDGMENTS

I love you, Danny. Thanks for all your support and help in writing this book. I love you, Elliot, Hazel, and Clifford. Thanks for coming along with me on several trips to Universal Parks this year.

Thanks to my parents, Karen and Jeff Peterson, and my in-laws, Tricia and Rick Craft, for always rallying behind me.

Tricia Craft and Emily Goodsell, you make me feel so much more confident in my work because you improve it so much! Thank you.

Special thank you to my brother, Brett, for coming along on an epic Universal research trip this year and for being up for anything, including riding the ludicrous VelociCoaster. Also, another thank you to my parents, Jeff and Karen, for coming along to the opposite coast to do an incredible day at Universal Studios Hollywood with me.

Joe Perry, thanks for being on my team. I cannot believe this is our *fourth* book together!

And to Julia Jacques, Sarah Doughty, and Mary Kate Schulte at Adams Media for trusting in my visions and creativity and allowing me to branch out into new subjects.

PREFACE

In summer 2010, The Wizarding World of Harry Potter: Hogsmeade opened in Islands of Adventure at Universal Orlando Resort. When I got to visit in early 2011, the sight brought tears to my eyes. Universal had truly captured the magic of Harry Potter from the books and movies in a physical location that I could visit.

My family and I visit Universal Studios Hollywood and Universal Orlando Resort each year and have been blown away by the tastiness and high quality of their foods and drinks over the course of our travels. These are not your stereotypical theme park offerings; these are delicious eats and sips that also incorporate the Parks' unique intellectual properties. In addition to the beloved Harry Potter franchise, these properties include The Simpsons and Nickelodeon. I knew I had to publish a book of recipes for the incredible foods and drinks inspired by these worlds and characters, so that everyone can have the magic of Universal Parks in their own kitchens whenever they want them. I hope you'll love these recipes and feel my passion for these Parks in each and every one!

INTRODUCTION

The Big Pink, Who Hash, Fever Fudge—these are just a few of the tantalizing recipes offered at Universal Theme Parks. Of course, you may not have a trip planned to Universal just yet. Or maybe you're an annual visitor but want to prep your taste buds for all the treats you'll soon be enjoying. The Parks span all the greatest Universal properties (like Harry Potter, Jurassic Park, The Simpsons, Minions, and Dr. Seuss) and everything in between, but you don't have to wait to visit the Parks to get your hands on these yummies.

The Unofficial Universal Theme Parks Cookbook contains more than seventy-five of the most iconic foods and drinks from both the California and Florida Universal Parks. Organized by course, this book provides easy-to-make recipes so you can whip up a little movie magic right in your home. You'll find:

- Breakfasts and pastries to start your morning out right, like The Big Pink donut served in Springfield and the Child Traditional English Breakfast from Three Broomsticks
- Appetizers, small bites, and snacks, like the super-popular Pizza-Stuffed Pretzels from Carmen's Veranda and sweet Korean Corn Dogs from Mummy Eats
- Satisfying entrées such as Cottage Pie from the Leaky Cauldron and a vegan Slow-Roasted Mojo Jackfruit from Jurassic Cafe

- Sugar confections galore, including everything in the Skiving Snackboxes at Weasleys' Wizard Wheezes and Blue Camo Fudge from San Francisco Candy Factory
- Mouthwatering desserts, including Lavender Blueberry Panna Cotta from Mythos Restaurant and Nutella Banana Pudding from Minion Cafe
- And all the drinks you could ask for, like Pumpkin Juice from Hog's Head and Goose Juice from the world of Dr. Seuss

There are quick bites you can mix up in no time as well as more impressive dishes to wow your family or guests.

But before you put on that Minions apron, make sure you check out Part 1 for more details on the Universal worlds and characters you will explore in the recipes, as well as the kitchen tools and supplies you'll want to have on hand. Even a seasoned chef benefits from a little prep work.

Ready to roll camera? The properties of Universal Theme Parks are waiting to come to life in the form of delicious foods and satisfying sips. Lights, camera, action!

UNIVERSAL PARKS FOODS 101

Welcome to the cinematic world of Universal! Whether you've been to Universal Parks a ton of times, never visited before, or are just a fan of Universal's properties, there are always delicious dishes and drinks to discover.

In this part, you'll explore all the most iconic and popular foods and drinks served across all four US Universal Parks: Universal Studios Hollywood, Universal Studios Florida, Islands of Adventure, and Volcano Bay. Chapter 1 gets you all warmed up for the recipes in Part 2, with interesting background information about Universal Parks and their foods and drinks, as well as a look into their culinary future. You'll learn about the influence of the Harry Potter series, unique challenges posed with certain franchises, and more. And to prep you (and your kitchen) for creating the recipes, Chapter 2 details all the equipment you will want to have on hand. So let's dive into the magical world of Universal Theme Parks!

CHAPTER 1

UNIVERSAL OF YESTERDAY AND TODAY

Unlike most other theme and amusement parks, Universal has lived an incredibly long life and has grown through different uses and iterations of its Parks. Throughout all this time, people's desires have changed, including which movie and TV properties they love most and want to see come to life within Universal's gates. And with these changes come culinary shifts as well, with the Parks adapting flavors, colors, and more to create dishes and beverages befitting the films and series fans know and love.

In this chapter, you will explore Universal Parks and Resorts and how they and their menus have evolved over time. Before you bust out the mixing bowls, read on to learn more about the history of Universal and how today's beloved Theme Parks came to be, as well as what inspired the recipes you will explore in Part 2 of this book.

Universal Parks History

Universal Pictures began as a film studio back in 1912, producing movies on their Hollywood back lot in Studio City, California. It only took three years for executives to realize that there was more magic in the movies than just watching them in the theaters—people enjoyed seeing how they were made. So, they opened their doors to the public beginning in 1915. Curious onlookers would board tram cars and get whisked around the real Hollywood back lot. Admission was a whopping twenty-five cents and included a boxed lunch for an extra nickel.

Unfortunately, the exciting advent of "talkie" films (films that had sound) in the 1930s killed the back lot tour, as trams and noisy guests were ruining the film soundtracks. It wasn't until the summer of 1964 that Universal Studios Hollywood officially reopened its back lot to guests. Throughout the next few decades, back lot availability continued to wax and wane with the constant changes in technology.

Universal executives eventually decided to control the narrative themselves by adding staged experiences to the tour, like the Flash Flood that seemed almost real enough to wash the tram away! And in 1991, Universal Studios Hollywood's first "dark ride" (an attraction with a vehicle that points riders to story elements in an indoor show building), E.T. Adventure, opened to the public.

Just one year prior, in 1990, Universal Studios Florida had opened its gates and changed what Universal Parks were. While Universal Studios Hollywood began as a working studio with a small regard to theme park rides, Universal Studios Florida was born as a rival to Disney Parks and as an amusement epicenter. Staying true to its film heritage, Universal adopted the tagline "ride the movies" to show the blending of the films with heart-pounding rides.

Universal Expands

By the early 1990s, Universal Studios Florida was garnering great success and truly went toe to toe against Disney-MGM Studios (which had opened in 1989). In order to battle Disney at a larger level, Universal Parks in Florida expanded with a new Park called Islands of Adventure. This Park opened in 1999 and was set up with a central lagoon and various "islands" dotting the shores around the lagoon, including Seuss Landing, Jurassic Park, and Marvel Super Hero Island. This new Park allowed guests to spend their entire vacation at Universal, not just a one-day stopover. And one thing Universal had a leg up on over Disney was thrills. While Disney touted itself as a family-friendly vacation, Universal Parks wanted to appeal to teens and adults looking for a few more loop-the-loops.

Eventually Volcano Bay was also added to Universal's Florida lineup, and although it is a water park, Universal likes to consider it a water *theme* park because of its advanced ride technology, expansive selection, and overall storytelling. It really is very different from your typical water park and deserves to be in a category all its own.

At the time of this writing, Universal's Epic Universe is under construction as part of the Universal Orlando Resort and slated to open in 2025. It promises to bring even more favorite franchises to life, including an entire Nintendo section.

Of course, the United States is not the only country that hosts Universal Theme Parks. In fact, there are Universal Parks in Japan, Singapore, and Beijing. So, if you find yourself in any of those locations, check out the exciting attractions and shows those Parks have to offer!

Making IPs Into Parks

Since Universal began as a movie studio, it seems obvious that its Parks would focus on its valuable IPs (intellectual properties). Some iconic properties you may have heard of that are featured at the Parks include Jurassic Park, King Kong, The Simpsons, Men in Black, Jaws, The Mummy, and The Fast and the Furious, and there are many more. All these properties have not only brought in big bucks at the box office, but also thrill millions of guests every year with their theme park attractions. You can crash down a raging waterfall while escaping a T. rex on Jurassic Park River Adventure and take out aliens as they pop out from all angles on Men in Black Alien Attack. At Universal, *you* get to live out your fan fantasies by jumping right into the attractions based on the pictures you grew up with or currently love.

The Acquisition of Harry Potter

One Universal IP that stands out and has gripped the world is Harry Potter. Seven books turned into eight movies that seemed to define a generation—introducing the franchise to a theme park seemed an obvious choice. But Harry Potter wasn't produced by Universal Pictures; it was made by Warner Bros. And Warner Bros. doesn't have a theme park in the United States. So, which Parks would get to have Harry Potter grace their gates? Both Universal and Disney placed bids to bring Harry to life, with Disney proposing a corner of Fantasyland to include a couple Harry Potter attractions and a shop and restaurant. Universal laid out a full-sized land that would pluck the streets of Hogsmeade and grounds of Hogwarts from the novels and movies and make them tangible, with several shops, restaurants, rides, and shows. Universal got the deal and got to work building one of the most ambitious theme park projects to date. In 2010, the land was opened.

After the wild success of Hogsmeade in Islands of Adventure, Universal announced that a second Harry Potter land would be built in Universal Studios Florida and embody Diagon Alley, the shopping and dining district of The Wizarding World. Opened in 2014, this second land connects to Hogsmeade via the Hogwarts Express—a real locomotive that whisks guests from one world to the next.

Diving Into Food and Drinks, Headfirst

From the candies Harry Potter and his friends purchase at Honeydukes to the tropical fare guests might enjoy after following a herd of brachiosaurs to treats resembling the beloved Minions, creators at Universal wanted the Park attractions dedicated to its intellectual properties to offer foods and drinks that would resonate with fans. And they delivered. Among the main properties in Universal are Harry Potter, The Simpsons, Jurassic Park, Minions and Despicable Me, Dr. Seuss, and The Mummy. Each location dedicated to these franchises offers meals, snacks, desserts, and/or drinks that delight Parkgoers of all ages.

HARRY POTTER

The Wizarding World of Harry Potter brought not only expectations of sights, sounds, smells, and thrills but also of tastes. Potterheads needed the food and beverages in The Wizarding World to match what they expected from page and screen. The stakes were extremely high.

Universal didn't disappoint. The Wizarding World is full of foods and drinks that are just as captivating as the attractions in the Park. Dishes like Fish and Chips, Pumpkin Pasties, and Child Traditional English Breakfast bring the feeling of Britain to Florida and California in each bite. Fans can enjoy Fever Fudge, Puking Pastilles, Pumpkin Juice, and other treats mentioned in the books and movies.

The culinary experiences of The Wizarding World proved just how important it was that the food and drinks across Universal Parks were as immersive as the IPs themselves.

THE SIMPSONS

Universal chefs had the opposite problem from The Wizarding World when creating menus for Springfield (the world of The Simpsons). Harry Potter food had to live up to what fans craved from the books and movies, but Simpsons fans were afraid there wouldn't be anything yummy to eat in Springfield. *The Simpsons* is known for tongue-in-cheek, irreverent comedy that often includes food jokes centered around interesting, even bizarre, dishes and drinks and puzzling ingredients. Recipes from the show like Chicken Thumbs, Krusty Burger, Flaming Moe, and more needed to be served up in the Parks as not only edible, but delectable. The skilled chefs created incredible dishes that hearken to the feel of *The Simpsons* while being absolutely tasty. At least they had one easy task to look forward to during their creations: making The Big Pink donut! Who doesn't want to hold up a brightly frosted donut as big as their head in front of the famous Lard Lad statue?

JURASSIC PARK

Jurassic Park was another challenge separate from the others: The Jurassic Park and Jurassic World film series are not known for their foods. While there is a plethora of information on the franchise in the form of several books and six films, characters rarely—if ever—take a moment to eat something while they are, well, being eaten. Chefs needed to imagine the kinds of foods that would be served in Jurassic Park, and for that, they mostly drew on inspiration from where Jurassic Park would be geographically located, near Costa Rica. Many of the dishes served up in these sections of Universal are Latin American and have succulent pork, chicken, and plantains served with heaping portions of rice and beans. And who could forget to grab a Tiki Tai from Isla Nu-Bar before going on the Jurassic Park River Adventure?!

MINIONS AND DESPICABLE ME

Universal Studios Hollywood, although the first Universal Park created, has tended to just adopt rides and experiences that do well in Florida, like Hogsmeade. But there is one area of Universal Studios Hollywood that isn't found in the Florida Parks, and that is the "Super Silly Fun Land" of Minions and Despicable Me. It encompasses two attractions, two play areas, multiple carnival-style games, and a delicious eatery. Minion Cafe boasts tasty eats and eye-popping treats inspired by characters and items from the films, like Unicorn Cupcakes and Nutella Banana Pudding. And it often sells specialty cups and popcorn buckets seasonally, so be sure to check inside each time you visit to add to your Minion merchandise collection.

DR. SEUSS

Seuss Landing needed no prodding to get going in regard to cuisine: Many Dr. Seuss books include food and drinks. Who hasn't read *Green Eggs and Ham* and wondered if the dish was actually yummy? What did you imagine Moose Juice and Goose Juice would taste like as you read *Dr. Seuss's Sleep Book*? The offerings in Seuss Landing answer your pressing questions about Seuss recipes. Every dish and drink is colorful and unique, just like the pages of the books they were born in.

THE MUMMY

The original Mummy was a classic Universal Pictures monster, included with the likes of Frankenstein's Monster, Dracula, and the Creature from the Black Lagoon. But in 1999, Universal resurrected the monster in a new way with the film series starring Brendan Fraser. They revived it again in 2017 with Tom Cruise at the helm. We are lucky this creature just won't die, because the rides and foods that have come out at the Parks thanks to the films have been wonderful. Mummy Eats at Universal Studios Hollywood serves up tasty and fresh corn dogs, churros, and fries with ice-cold cups of soda.

SPOT THE FRANCHISE

To make it easier to locate recipes from these main intellectual properties in this book, you will find a special icon beside each relevant recipe in Part 2. Look for these icons as you flip through the recipes:

| Harry Potter | The Simpsons | Jurassic Park | Minions and Despicable Me | Dr. Seuss | The Mummy |

A Myriad of Choices for a Myriad of People

If you build a theme park with everyone's favorite properties turned into rides and shows, guests are going to come—not only from nearby, but from around the globe. Universal Parks have visitors each day who have traveled hours and days to get there, and when they get there, they will be *hungry* and *thirsty*. Imagine you are throwing a dinner party and you've invited one hundred friends from around the world to attend, and they are all the pickiest eaters ever. What do you serve?

How do you even begin? This is the task that Universal chefs are given, to satiate and delight not just some people, but *everyone*. Because of this, you'll notice that there isn't just one type of food offered across the Parks, but a wide array of choices that are sure to please even the pickiest of palates.

Take the breakfast offerings at the Leaky Cauldron as an example. The Leaky Cauldron is set in Wizarding London and, as such, should offer British food. However, not everyone is partial to a plate of beans and half a tomato first thing in the morning. So, to please more people, the restaurant also offers an American Breakfast (eggs, potatoes, bacon, and sausage) and a Pancake Breakfast (pancakes, bacon, and sausage). Maybe the fictional Leaky Cauldron wouldn't serve those items, but when a hungry toddler shows up at 8 a.m., sticking their nose up at beans, even the most fanatical Potterheads will tip their pointed hats to the chefs who had the foresight to look out for everyone.

As another example, look to the Jurassic Park section of Islands of Adventure. Most of the food is inspired by Central and South American cuisine, but you'll notice Pizza Predattoria, where travelers and Floridians alike can find slices of pizza and sandwiches if Latin American food isn't their thing. Making sure each section of the Parks has a variety of food and beverage options comes first; the theming wraps around those dishes.

Universal Parks Food and You

Before now, you had to go to a Universal Theme Park to partake of the delicious meals, snacks, and drinks of your favorite Universal properties. But with the recipes in this book, Universal Parks foods and sips can be part of your everyday life! Start your morning with Overnight Oats or Pumpkin Pasties. Or enjoy a delicious lunch of a Pizza-Stuffed Pretzel or a can of Who Hash paired with a cold glass of Moose Juice.

Or maybe you are looking for something to serve for a special occasion. The dishes in this book are perfectly designed to bring to the next movie-release party—or you can host one yourself. All the treats you need for a Jurassic Park movie marathon, Dr. Seuss event at the elementary school, or magical Harry Potter party can be found here. At Universal Parks, you can "ride the movies," but with this book, you can now "taste the movies" too—right in your own home!

CHAPTER 2

THE UNIVERSAL PARKS COOK'S ESSENTIALS

It's about time to get cooking! But before you pick up that pan, take a look through this chapter to make sure your kitchen is stocked with the tools to make edible movie magic. Most of the recipes ahead require very little in the way of specialty equipment, but some recipes differ in what they will require. The tools used in Part 2 are listed alphabetically in this chapter, so you can also flip back to a specific section at any time while cooking or baking.

If you don't own some of the supplies and tools, there may be substitutions you can use instead. This chapter (and recipe tips in Part 2) includes some alternate methods and appliances, and you may also find additional ideas with a quick online search. Once you've familiarized yourself with the essentials for a kitchen brimming with Universal wonder, it'll be full speed ahead to the recipes!

Tools and Pantry Staples

The world of Universal Parks goodies awaits—once you're armed with the essentials, of course. This section provides more detail about each appliance and special pantry item used in Part 2.

AIR FRYER

An air fryer is a compact mini oven that can reach high temperatures and circulate heat quickly in order to crisp up foods, giving them a "fried" taste. If you don't have an air fryer, that's okay! Just use your standard oven and cook as instructed. You may need to add more time, so keep an eye on the food as it cooks.

BAKING SHEETS

Baking sheets come in many shapes and sizes, but the best ones for the recipes in this book have ½"-tall sides and are called "half sheets."

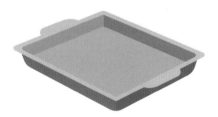

BLENDER

A good-quality, high-powered stand blender will help you achieve a smoother consistency for smoothies and dips. Start with a low setting and turn up the speed as larger pieces break up.

BUNDTLETTE PAN

A Bundtlette pan is a *mini* Bundt pan and is used to make the Pumpkin Cake. Bundtlette pans can be purchased from online retailers. If you do not have access to a Bundtlette pan, use a mini muffin pan and bake the cakes for 2 additional minutes to cook through.

CHOCOLATE COMB

If you aren't a chocolate connoisseur, this may not be in your kitchen arsenal yet. Search online retailers for a chocolate comb or cake scraper and look for one with matching square "teeth" to create a striped shape when pulled over chocolate. This tool is used in the recipe for Signature Key Lime Cheesecake in making the chocolate curls.

COCKTAIL SHAKER

This makes mixing easy for mixed drinks, especially if a thicker syrup is used. You can also quickly chill a drink during mixing by adding ice to the shaker beforehand. If you don't have a cocktail shaker, just whisk the mixture well in a large glass or small bowl and strain through a sieve.

COOLING RACK

A common wire cooling/drying rack is sufficient for the recipes in this book. They are typically made from stainless steel and have straight lines or a crosshatch pattern.

COTTON CANDY MACHINE

You don't need to invest in a machine you see at a carnival to make great cotton candy at home. Big-box stores and online retailers carry low-cost machines that can make good cotton candy in smaller volumes.

ELECTRIC PRESSURE COOKER

Electric pressure cookers can save a lot of time in the kitchen and provide a delicious product. Many different brands are available. Make sure that there is a properly sized inner pot placed in the cooker and that you are careful to avoid steam burns when you release pressure from the pot.

FOOD COLORING

Many of the recipes in this book use food coloring to pull off the original look found in the Parks. Gel colors are always preferred for solid foods and liquid colors for drinks. Gel colors have a brighter pop of color than liquid food coloring, and the tighter consistency means they won't change the texture of the dish. If your gel colors come in pots and cannot be added in drops, dip a wooden toothpick into the gel and swipe it through the food you want to color. Repeat for each drop needed.

FOOD PROCESSOR

Food processors are basically high-powered blenders that specialize in chopping dry ingredients. If you don't have a food processor, a blender works just fine. If you have neither, chopping very finely with a knife works too—it is just more labor-intensive and less uniform.

GLASS PANS

Several recipes in this book use glass pans. Metal pans can be substituted; just be sure to check the food more often to prevent overcooking.

GRILL OR GRILL PAN

For items that need to be grilled, an outdoor grill and indoor stove-top grill pan are interchangeable. Propane grills should be preheated to ensure even cooking. Indoor grill pans need to be greased with cooking oil before use to help prevent sticking. Charcoal grills can also be used; they just require more prep and cleanup. Consult your grill instructions for safety guidelines.

ICE CREAM MACHINE

The easiest ice cream machines to use are the ones with freezable bowls. The bowl is removed from the freezer moments before use, and cream or drink mix is poured directly into the frozen bowl. The bowl then spins on a base, and a paddle mixes and scrapes the inside. Follow the manufacturer instructions to run the machine until the consistency matches the recipe description. Other options are available if you are unable to use this type of ice cream machine. For example, you can use a bucket-type ice cream machine that requires ice cubes and rock salt. Just pour the mixture from the recipe into the metal inner container and fill the outer bucket with ice and rock salt. As with ice cream machines that use freezable bowls, run the machine according to the manufacturer's instructions until the consistency matches the recipe description.

ICE POP MOLDS

You'll need an ice pop mold for the Sundaes on a Stick recipe. Plastic ice pop molds are inexpensive and can be found in most grocery or big-box stores. However, if you don't have one, you can use small plastic or paper cups instead. Simply pour the mixture in and cover the cup with aluminum foil. Push an ice pop stick through the foil in the center of the cup. The foil will stabilize the stick and keep it in the center as the mixture freezes.

IMMERSION BLENDER

Immersion blenders are convenient because you can leave your soup or sauce in the pot on the stove and purée it, rather than moving it to a stand blender or food processor. If you don't have an immersion blender, however, a stand blender or food processor will work just as well.

MINI BUNDT PAN

A mini Bundt pan is used to make the Lemon Poppy Bundts. The shape allows for even cooking and a well for sauce to be poured if desired. Pans made of silicone are best because they can be twisted and pushed to release the cakes. If you don't have a mini Bundt pan, one can be purchased online.

MOLDS

Some recipes in this book require the use of molds, especially in candy making. Silicone or plastic molds will work fine; just make sure plastic ones are rated to withstand the temperatures of hot candy and won't melt when poured into.

MUFFIN PANS

Common muffin pans have six or twelve divots per pan. Generously grease the pan with nonstick cooking oil or spray to prevent sticking.

PARCHMENT PAPER

Almost every recipe in this book that requires baking will instruct you to line your baking sheet or pan with parchment paper. This simple step ensures a more even baking surface and more consistent browning, and it greatly reduces the likelihood of your food sticking to the pan. Parchment paper can be found in any grocery store.

PIE PAN

A 9" pie pan is used to make the Mile High Apple Pie. A glass or aluminum pan will work equally well. Be sure to grease the pan generously with nonstick cooking oil or spray to avoid sticking.

PIPING BAGS

Many recipes in this book call for piping bags, but you don't need a fancy set. A heavy-duty plastic sandwich or gallon bag will do. Simply load the dough, frosting, or other mixture into the bag, then snip a small edge off one of the bottom corners. Start your hole out small and make it bigger as needed. (Some recipes in this book call for special piping bag tips. While you don't *need* to use a piping bag tip for any recipe, it can make for an eye-catching design.)

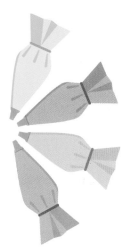

POTS AND PANS

Heavy-bottomed saucepans are preferred in many recipes in this book. The thick metal bottom regulates the temperature better and prevents burning. If you don't have heavy-bottomed pans, any appropriately sized pot or pan will do; just keep an extra-close eye on foods cooking on the stove. Stir more frequently to prevent burning. Nonstick pans are not usually necessary but are helpful in some recipes, such as the various crepes. The nonstick surface allows the food to slide off without sticking. If you don't have a nonstick pan, use plenty of nonstick cooking oil or spray to grease the pan before cooking.

RAMEKINS

"Ramekin" is just a fancy word for a small glass or ceramic bowl that can be baked in the oven. If you don't have designated ramekins, check the bottoms of your small glass storage containers or bowls to see if they are oven safe.

RICE COOKER

Rice cookers are common and can range from simple and inexpensive to luxurious and pricey. A rice cooker is used in the recipe for Coconut Curry Chicken in this book. If you don't already have a rice cooker and would prefer not to buy one, simply follow the instructions on rice packaging to make on the stovetop instead.

ROLLING PIN

Rolling pins come in many shapes and sizes, including those that have handles on the sides, the French style (a simple wooden dowel), and the straight, cylindrical style. Any variety is fine for use in the recipes in this book.

SIEVE

The sieves described in the recipes in this book refer to a stainless-steel, mesh, half-dome strainer. Get one with a fine-mesh or medium-mesh sieve.

SLOW COOKER

A slow cooker is used in the recipe for Mango BBQ Pulled Pork Sandwiches in this book, to slowly cook and tenderize the pork. If you don't have a slow cooker already, they can be easily found in most grocery and big-box stores, or online. Thrift stores are a good place to look for one on the cheap.

SPRINGFORM PAN

A springform pan is needed to make the Signature Key Lime Cheesecake in this book. This is a special type of pan that hugs the cake around the outside and can be unlatched to release the cake. It be found at most stores that sell kitchen supplies, or online.

STAND MIXER

Many of the recipes in this book that require mixing call for a stand mixer. This machine makes mixing, whipping, and kneading easy and uniform. If you don't have a stand mixer, the second-best option is a hand mixer. These often also have interchangeable attachments for mixing or whipping. If you have neither, of course you can mix, whip, and knead by hand—it will just require a bit more strength and stamina.

SYRUPS

Syrups are a key part of making many mixed drinks. Brands like Monin or Torani are usually easy to find in stores or at online retailers. If you can't find Monin or Torani syrups, other brands work just as well.

THERMOMETERS

A confection or candy thermometer is essential for any candy making or deep-frying. Bringing mixtures to the correct temperature determines the final product's texture and taste. A meat thermometer is crucial when assuring that meat is cooked to a safe temperature. Both types of thermometers can be bought at most grocery and big-box stores.

Getting Started

This chapter has covered a lot of information, but don't fret! The following recipes were designed with the beginner cook in mind; no matter your skill level, you can make these recipes! Read through the recipe you're going to tackle in its entirety before getting started so you'll know what equipment you need. Revisit this chapter at any time for a quick refresher. And that's it—you're ready to begin!

PART 2

UNIVERSAL PARKS RECIPES

Now that all the business is out of the way, you are ready to get cooking! The following part holds the secrets to amazing Universal flavors. The next six chapters are filled with more than seventy-five recipes for foods and drinks from all four US Universal Theme Parks. Inspired by all your favorite characters and stories, from Harry Potter to Jurassic Park to The Simpsons, each page will have your mouth watering.

The chapters in this part are organized by cuisine type: Breakfasts and Pastries, Appetizers and Snacks, Entrées, Sugar Confections, Desserts, and Drinks. You can flip to a specific chapter to whatever recipes stand out; get direction from the Contents section at the front of this book; or cook, bake, and mix your way through every Park favorite. You can also start with something you've sampled in the past, something you've always been dying to try, or something you've never heard of before! Any way you use this book is up to you. Let's see what you whip up!

CHAPTER 3

BREAKFASTS AND PASTRIES

Whether you are spending your day at a Universal Park, or at home, breakfast is widely regarded as the most important meal of the day. It gives you the fuel you need when walking around a Park, running errands, or enjoying time with the family in your home.

In this chapter, you will discover great breakfast options served at Universal that you can whip up in your own kitchen. Whether you are in the mood for a healthier option like Egg White Florentine or Overnight Oats, want to treat yourself to something more indulgent like The Big Pink or Cinnamon Sugar Cruffins, or need an on-the-go bite like a Strawberry and Cheese Pop Tart or Pumpkin Pasties, this chapter has got you covered. And don't feel constrained to only eat these yummies in the morning—you can enjoy them any time of day! (Breakfast for dinner, anyone?) You decide in your home, so let's get cooking.

EGG WHITE FLORENTINE

Today *Cafe, Universal Studios Florida*

....

Universal is owned by NBC, and the *Today* show is aired on NBC networks—hence *Today* Cafe at Universal Studios Florida! Packed with delicious and healthful ingredients, the Egg White Florentine served here is a perfect portable breakfast to take on the go, whether you're at Universal Studios Florida or on your daily commute. Round out the dish with a bright fruit cup.

SERVES 1

- 1 (6") ciabatta roll, halved lengthwise
- 2 tablespoons olive oil
- 2 tablespoons basil pesto
- 4 large egg whites
- ½ teaspoon salt
- ¼ teaspoon ground black pepper
- 2 slices medium-sharp Cheddar cheese
- 2 tablespoons tomato sauce
- ¼ cup fresh baby spinach

1. Preheat a nonstick skillet over medium heat. Drizzle each cut-side ciabatta half with olive oil. Place oil side down into skillet and toast 1–3 minutes until light brown. Remove from pan and brush cut side of bottom half of roll with pesto. Set aside.
2. Mix egg whites, salt, and pepper in a small bowl, then pour into skillet. Cook 1–3 minutes until bottom is cooked, then flip and cook 1–3 more minutes until cooked through.
3. Fold eggs and place on top of pesto layer. Add cheese directly onto hot eggs. Spoon tomato sauce onto cheese and spread spinach on top of tomato sauce. Finish by placing top half of ciabatta onto spinach and slice in half widthwise on a diagonal. Serve immediately.

 **COOKING TIP**

This sandwich can be made in bulk ahead of time for the week. Just prepare as normal (increasing the recipe to make more sandwiches) and then wrap sandwiches tightly in wax paper and place into a freezer zip-top bag. Freeze up to one week, and move a sandwich to the refrigerator the night before you want to eat it. In the morning, microwave in the wax paper for about 1–2 minutes per side or until warmed through.

CINNAMON SUGAR CRUFFINS

Today *Cafe, Universal Studios Florida*

....

You might be wondering: What is a cruffin? First served in Melbourne, Australia, in 2013, a cruffin is an adorably shaped pastry full of flaky layers—a croissant baked in a muffin tin. Pull apart the layers and eat each one separately, or take a big bite through all the layers at once! Either way, each morsel will be packed with buttery flavor and cinnamon sugar goodness.

YIELDS 8 CRUFFINS

1 (16.3-ounce) package canned biscuit dough
10 tablespoons cinnamon sugar, divided
2 tablespoons salted butter, melted

1. Preheat oven to 350°F. Coat a muffin tin with nonstick cooking spray and set aside.
2. Working with one piece of dough at a time, fold biscuit dough in half, then use a rolling pin to flatten into a long rectangle (about 2" × 8"). Sprinkle evenly with 1 tablespoon cinnamon sugar, then roll tightly from one end to the other. Place into prepared muffin tin fold side down. Repeat with remaining dough.
3. Bake 15–20 minutes until tops are deep brown. Remove from oven and brush with melted butter and sprinkle with remaining 2 tablespoons cinnamon sugar. Allow to cool in pan 5 minutes before serving.

OVERNIGHT OATS

Today *Cafe, Universal Studios Florida*

....

Today Cafe is directly inside the entrance of Universal Studios Florida, in a perfect location to grab some breakfast before starting out on your fun-filled day. While *Today* Cafe serves its Overnight Oats with seasonal berries, almonds, and coconut, you can use whatever you like, including banana slices, walnuts, raspberries, or chocolate chips if you prefer!

SERVES 1

½ cup rolled oats
½ cup whole milk
½ cup honey-vanilla whole-milk Greek yogurt
1 tablespoon chia seeds
1 tablespoon pure honey
1 fresh strawberry, hulled and sliced
2 tablespoons fresh blueberries
2 tablespoons slivered almonds
2 tablespoons toasted coconut

1. Add oats, milk, yogurt, chia seeds, and honey to a sealable jar or container and stir to combine. Let set in refrigerator at least 4 hours, up to overnight.
2. Remove from refrigerator, scoop into a bowl, and stir, then top with strawberry slices, blueberries, almonds, and coconut in straight lines across the top of oats. Enjoy immediately.

VEGAN ELDERBERRY CROISSANTS

Today Cafe, Universal Studios Florida

....

Everyone likes a buttery, flaky croissant, but not everyone loves the actual butter, so Universal offers many dishes that are lifestyle- or allergy-friendly, including many vegan options. Making croissant dough from scratch is painstaking, but fortunately, refrigerated crescent roll dough already comes vegan! Now all you must do is add a little elderberry jam and bake, and you'll have delicious dairy-free croissants to enjoy.

SERVES 2

1 (8-ounce) package canned vegan crescent roll dough
4 tablespoons elderberry jam

1. Preheat oven to 375°F and line a baking sheet with parchment paper.
2. Unroll dough and pinch all seams together to create one large sheet of dough. Cut across the long diagonal to create two large triangles. Place 2 tablespoons elderberry jam on each triangle and spread without getting too close to edges. Roll into a croissant, starting at the base and ending with the point. Place both rolls on prepared baking sheet.
3. Bake 15-20 minutes until tops are deep brown. Remove from oven and allow to cool on baking sheet 10 minutes.

 **MIX IT UP**

If you don't have any elderberry jam around (or prefer another flavor), feel free to use your favorite jam flavor instead. This dish works just as well with strawberry, grape, or mango jam!

RASPBERRY AND PASSION FRUIT CREAM CREPES

Central Park Crêpes, Universal Studios Florida

....

Crepes are the ultimate changeable food item. Just as comfortable savory or sweet, these neutrally flavored and ultra-thin pancakes can become whatever you want them to be. This particular variety is a creamy, fruity blend that could be a snack, dessert, or breakfast. Look to Chapter 4 for a savory alternative, also served at Central Park Crêpes, called Smoked Brisket Crepes.

SERVES 4

FOR CREPES
1 cup all-purpose flour
2 cups whole milk
4 large egg whites
1 tablespoon vegetable oil
1 tablespoon pure honey
½ teaspoon salt

FOR PASSION FRUIT CREAM
1 cup heavy whipping cream
2 tablespoons passion fruit
  syrup

1. To make Crepes: In a blender, add all ingredients and blend until well combined, about 30 seconds. Heat a large nonstick frying pan over medium heat 30 seconds. Coat pan with nonstick cooking spray. Pour ¼–½ cup batter directly from blender into center of pan, swirling pan while you pour, to fill pan with a thin layer of batter. Cook about 1½ minutes. Once the edges are brown and pulling away from the sides, slide a rubber spatula around the entire edge of the batter, slip spatula under the Crepe, and flip. Cook an additional 1½ minutes on the other side. Remove to a large plate.

2. Repeat cooking with remaining batter, spraying pan between each Crepe.

3. To make Passion Fruit Cream: Add all ingredients to the bowl of a stand mixer fitted with a whisk attachment. Whisk on low speed until mixture is light and fluffy and has stiff peaks, 2–4 minutes.

(continued on next page)

FOR ASSEMBLY

4 unfrosted red velvet
   cupcakes, cut into
   8 pieces each
1 cup fresh raspberries
4 teaspoons cinnamon sugar

4. To Assemble: Lay out 1 Crepe on a serving plate. In the center, smear a generous portion—about ¼ cup—Passion Fruit Cream in a line. Add ¼ of red velvet cupcake pieces and sprinkle with ¼ cup fresh raspberries. Fold Crepe in half over ingredients, then roll to create a cone shape. Dollop a little more Passion Fruit Cream on top of the cone and sprinkle with 1 teaspoon cinnamon sugar. Repeat with remaining Crepes, Passion Fruit Cream, and toppings. Serve immediately.

SIMPLIFICATION HACK

A whipped cream dispenser can make Passion Fruit Cream in an instant! Not everyone has one of these in their kitchen, but if you do, it's a time-saver for sure. Just add heavy whipping cream and passion fruit syrup to the canister, add the charging cartridge, and bam—you've got fluffy whipped cream on tap.

THE BIG PINK

Lard Lad Donuts, Universal Studios Florida

Even if you've never seen an episode of *The Simpsons*, you've probably seen a picture of Homer Simpson holding a pink-frosted donut in his hand. The man and the donut are practically synonymous. And while Homer is usually seen holding an ordinary-sized donut, food creators at Universal wanted this offering to be anything *but* ordinary. Measuring 8" across, The Big Pink is sure to bring a huge smile to anyone's face. Share with family or friends (or eat it yourself if you'd like!), sliced into wedges like a cake. The soft insides and creamy frosting are addictive—just ask Homer.

YIELDS 6 DONUTS

FOR DONUTS
1¼ cups whole milk
1 (0.25-ounce) packet fast-rising instant yeast
2 large eggs
½ cup salted butter, softened
¼ cup granulated sugar
1 teaspoon salt
5 cups all-purpose flour
6 cups vegetable oil, for frying

1. To make Donuts: In a microwave-safe bowl, microwave milk in 30-second increments until milk is 100°F, stirring between cook times. Sprinkle yeast on top of milk and allow to bloom 10 minutes.

2. In the bowl of a stand mixer fitted with a dough hook, beat eggs, butter, sugar, and salt 2 minutes. Add yeast and milk mixture and beat 1 minute. Slowly add in flour, beating until fully incorporated and dough pulls away from the sides of the bowl. Then knead dough on low speed an additional 5 minutes.

3. Transfer dough to a large bowl greased with nonstick cooking spray, cover with a towel, and allow to rise in a warm place (like a sunny room or near a stove) until doubled in size, about 1 hour.

(continued on next page)

FOR FROSTING

2 cups confectioners' sugar
3 tablespoons whole milk
½ teaspoon vanilla extract
2 drops pink gel food
  coloring
6 tablespoons rainbow
  sprinkles

4. Turn dough out onto a floured surface and use a rolling pin to flatten to ½" thickness. Using an 8" circular pot or container lid as a guide, cut six 8" circles from the dough with a 1" center hole in each. If needed, re-roll remaining dough to make more circles.

5. Place dough on floured baking sheets, cover with towels, and allow to rise in a warm place 45 minutes.

6. Heat oil in a large pot over medium heat to 365°F. Line two baking sheets with paper towels and set aside. Maintain oil at 365°F while frying.

7. Fry Donuts one at a time for 1 minute per side until golden brown and cooked through. Remove to paper towel–lined baking sheets. Allow Donuts to cool completely, about 30 minutes.

8. To make Frosting: In a medium bowl, combine confectioners' sugar, milk, vanilla, and food coloring.

9. Gently spoon Frosting onto cooled Donuts until tops are covered. Sprinkle with rainbow sprinkles while still wet. Serve immediately.

HAM, EGG, AND CHEESE EMPANADAS

Croissant Moon Bakery, Islands of Adventure

. . . .

Just like a crepe, the empanada can be a vehicle for lots of different fillings. In fact, Pumpkin Pasties, also in this chapter, are similar: half-circle pastries with filling. At Croissant Moon Bakery, these delicious empanadas are served with a small cup of salsa for dipping. Each dish from this dining location is varied and eclectic to satisfy Parkgoer desires, whether for a simple breakfast or a smaller bite between meals.

YIELDS 6 EMPANADAS

1 (2-count) box refrigerated pie crusts
6 large eggs
2 tablespoons sour cream
½ teaspoon salt
½ teaspoon ground black pepper
¼ cup finely diced cooked ham
½ cup shredded medium-sharp Cheddar cheese

1. Preheat oven to 400°F. Line a baking sheet with parchment paper and set aside. Remove pie crusts from box and allow to sit on countertop 15 minutes.
2. Meanwhile, prepare the filling. Line a large plate with paper towels and set aside. Crack eggs into a medium bowl and add sour cream, salt, and pepper. Whisk until combined.
3. Heat a large nonstick pan over medium heat. Pour egg mixture into pan and stir until cooked (scrambled), 2–4 minutes.
4. Add ham and cheese and fold in. Pour scramble out onto paper towel–lined plate to drain.
5. Unroll pie crusts and use a 4" circular pot or container lid as a guide to cut three 4" circles out of each pie crust. Scoop about 2 tablespoons egg filling into middle of each circle, fold in half, and crimp with a fork to close. If crust isn't sticking, line inside of crust with a dab of water, then crimp.
6. Lay empanadas on prepared baking sheet and bake 15–20 minutes until golden brown. Allow to cool 10 minutes on baking sheet before serving.

STRAWBERRY AND CHEESE POP TARTS

Croissant Moon Bakery, Islands of Adventure

....

Can you buy a toaster pastry from the grocery store? Yes. Will it taste as flaky and fresh as these homemade ones? Probably not! Making homemade toaster pastries is quick, easy, and fun. This version is sold at Universal right at the entrance of Islands of Adventure at an adorable shop called Croissant Moon Bakery, a perfect placement that is excellent for grabbing breakfast before speed walking to the first attraction of the day.

SERVES 4

1 (2-count) box refrigerated pie crusts
4 tablespoons cream cheese, softened
4 tablespoons strawberry preserves
1 cup confectioners' sugar
1½ tablespoons whole milk
3 drops pink gel food coloring
4 tablespoons rainbow sprinkles

1. Preheat oven to 450°F. Line a baking sheet with parchment paper and set aside.
2. Unroll pie crusts and cut each crust into four rectangles about 3" × 4". Spread cream cheese onto four rectangles, then spread strawberry preserves on top of cream cheese, making sure to keep ½" along the edges clean. Rub water onto the clean margins and lay remaining four rectangles on top of the preserves. Crimp edges. Poke center of each pastry once with a fork to vent.
3. Bake on prepared sheet 10–14 minutes until lightly browned. Remove from oven and allow to cool completely on baking sheet, 30–45 minutes.
4. Combine confectioners' sugar, milk, and food coloring in a small bowl. Drizzle across each pastry and quickly cover with rainbow sprinkles. Allow frosting to harden, about 10 minutes, before serving.

GREEN EGGS AND HAM TOTS

Green Eggs and Ham Cafe, Islands of Adventure

In the popular book by Dr. Seuss, the main character doesn't want to try the dish green eggs and ham because of its peculiar look and because he's never tried it before. But—spoiler alert—he ends up trying the dish and loving it! Be just like him and give this interesting-looking recipe a try. You may never go back to plain old yellow scrambled eggs again. The addition of the pesto lends the eggs most of their green color (added gel coloring makes them pop) but also gives a fresh flavor that mixes well with the cheese and ham.

SERVES 1

2 cups frozen Tater Tots
3 large eggs
1 tablespoon basil pesto
1 drop green gel food
   coloring
¼ cup white queso
¼ cup diced warmed ham

1. Prepare Tater Tots according to package instructions and pour into a medium bowl.
2. Heat a medium nonstick pan over medium heat. Crack eggs into a separate small bowl and add pesto and food coloring. Mix, then pour into pan. Stir to scramble 2–4 minutes until cooked through.
3. Pour eggs onto cooked Tater Tots. Scoop queso into a small microwave-safe bowl and microwave 1 minute, stirring halfway through, until warmed. Drizzle queso onto eggs and sprinkle with ham. Serve immediately.

 **COOKING TIP**

This dish can easily be multiplied for a large crowd. Just add more ingredients for each person you are feeding. Serve it up in a large casserole dish and place it on the table or include it in a buffet line.

PUMPKIN PASTIES

Honeydukes, Islands of Adventure

When students ride the Hogwarts Express from Kings Cross station in London to Hogwarts castle in Scotland to begin the school year, a trolley of sweets, including delicious Pumpkin Pasties, is offered through the corridors. This treat is essentially a portable pumpkin pie and may become a new staple in your household—either in the fall or year-round!

SERVES 4

1 (2-count) box refrigerated pie crusts
1 cup canned pumpkin
½ teaspoon ground cinnamon
¼ teaspoon ground allspice
¼ teaspoon ground nutmeg
2 tablespoons granulated sugar
1 large egg, beaten

1. Preheat oven to 400°F. Line a baking sheet with parchment paper and set aside.
2. Unroll both pie crusts and use a 4" circular pot or container lid as a guide to cut four 4" circles from crusts. Discard scraps.
3. In a small bowl, combine pumpkin, cinnamon, allspice, nutmeg, and sugar. Spoon ¼ of mixture onto center of each circle. Wet edges with water, then fold circles in half over filling. Crimp with a fork. Poke fork once in top of each crust to vent.
4. Place pasties on prepared baking sheet and brush with beaten egg. Bake 15–20 minutes or until golden brown. Cool on baking sheet 1 hour, then serve.

CHILD TRADITIONAL ENGLISH BREAKFAST

Three Broomsticks, Islands of Adventure

What does breakfast look like in your country? A typical "American" breakfast may include pancakes, bacon or sausage, and eggs. In England, where much of the Harry Potter books and movies are set, a traditional breakfast looks a bit different. Bacon, sausage, and eggs are still there, but the addition of grilled tomato and baked beans, really sets it apart. Enjoy this recipe as you imagine you are about to start your day of shopping and hanging out with friends in snowy Hogsmeade during a break from school at Hogwarts.

SERVES 2

FOR BRITISH BAKED BEANS
1 tablespoon vegetable oil
½ small yellow onion, peeled and diced
2 teaspoons minced garlic
1 cup canned crushed tomatoes, including juice
3 tablespoons ketchup
1 teaspoon granulated sugar
½ teaspoon Worcestershire sauce
1 teaspoon salt
1 cup water, plus more if needed
2 cups drained and rinsed canned great northern beans

1. To make British Baked Beans: Preheat oven to 325°F.
2. Heat oil in a large ovenproof skillet over medium heat. Add onion and cook 5 minutes until soft. Add garlic and cook 1 minute.
3. Add crushed tomatoes, ketchup, sugar, Worcestershire sauce, and salt and stir to combine. Add 1 cup water. Remove from heat and blend with an immersion blender in skillet, or transfer mixture to a stand blender and blend.
4. If using stand blender, return mixture to pan. Add more water if needed to achieve desired consistency. Add in beans and stir to combine.

(continued on next page)

FOR BREAKFAST POTATOES

2 medium Yukon Gold
    potatoes, thinly sliced into
    rounds
1 tablespoon olive oil
1 teaspoon salt
¼ teaspoon ground black
    pepper

FOR SCRAMBLED EGGS

4 large eggs
1 tablespoon sour cream
1 teaspoon salt
½ teaspoon ground black
    pepper

FOR GRILLED TOMATO

2 tablespoons salted butter,
    divided
1 Roma tomato, halved
¼ cup panko bread crumbs

FOR ASSEMBLY

2 links cooked pork sausage
4 strips cooked bacon
2 cooked croissants, at room
    temperature

5. Bake 20 minutes uncovered.

6. To make Breakfast Potatoes: Toss all ingredients together in a small bowl. Place potatoes in a single layer in air fryer set at 400°F and cook 10 minutes, flipping potatoes halfway. Add more time if needed for desired consistency.

7. To make Scrambled Eggs: Heat a medium nonstick pan over medium heat. Add all ingredients to a small bowl and beat with a fork. Pour into pan and cook while stirring continuously until eggs pull together and are fully cooked, 3–5 minutes.

8. To make Grilled Tomato: Place 1 tablespoon butter in a nonstick pan over medium-high heat and melt. Add tomato halves cut side down and cook until they start to blacken, 2–4 minutes. Remove from pan and set aside.

9. Add remaining 1 tablespoon butter to same pan and melt, then add panko bread crumbs and stir 2 minutes to toast. Sprinkle toasted panko bread crumbs onto tomato halves.

10. To Assemble: Divide British Baked Beans, Breakfast Potatoes, Scrambled Eggs, and Grilled Tomato halves onto two plates (there may be extra beans; any leftovers can be stored in refrigerator up to 4 days). Add 1 sausage link, 2 bacon strips, and 1 croissant to each plate. Serve immediately.

BANANA CREME TARTS

Thunder Falls Terrace, Islands of Adventure

Loaded with tropical flavor, these Banana Creme Tarts from Thunder Falls Terrace bring the jungles of Isla Nublar right into your kitchen.

YIELDS 6 TARTS

FOR CRUSTS
1 (2-count) box refrigerated
   pie crusts

FOR PLANTAINS
2 fresh plantains, peeled
   and thinly sliced into
   6 lengthwise slices

FOR FILLING
1½ cups whole milk
1 (3.4-ounce) package instant
   banana pudding mix

FOR MERINGUE
4 large egg whites
¼ teaspoon cream of tartar
½ cup granulated sugar

1. To make Crusts: Allow pie crusts to sit at room temperature 45 minutes.
2. Preheat oven to 450°F. Grease a jumbo muffin tin with nonstick cooking spray. Set aside. Unroll pie crusts and cut out six 4" circles (three from each crust). Mold each crust into muffin divots and prick all over with a fork.
3. Bake Crusts 10–12 minutes until golden brown. Remove from oven and allow to cool completely in tin, 1–2 hours.
4. To make Plantains: Coat plantain slices with nonstick cooking spray on both sides and place in air fryer. Air fry at 360°F 4 minutes on each side or until Plantains are cooked and crispy. Allow to cool completely, 1 hour.
5. To make Filling: Pour milk into a medium bowl. Add banana pudding mix and stir to combine. Refrigerate 10 minutes.
6. To make Meringue: Beat egg whites in a large bowl until foamy, about 2 minutes, then add cream of tartar and sugar and beat until stiff peaks form, about 5 minutes. Fold ½ of Meringue into Filling and reserve remaining Meringue in the refrigerator, in a piping bag fitted with a flat tip, until ready to assemble tarts.
7. Remove Crusts from tin. Scoop ¼ cup Filling into each Crust. Add a layer of Meringue to each and top each with a Plantain slice. Serve immediately.

LEMON POPPY BUNDTS

French Street Bistro, Universal Studios Hollywood

....

You might not typically wake up in the morning and whip up a cake for breakfast, but you will want to make an exception with these adorable little Lemon Poppy Bundts. The bright lemon flavor and miniature presentation will transport you to a French cafe. If you don't have a mini Bundt pan, try making these in a muffin tin instead. Just bake for a few more minutes and check the middles often with a toothpick to see if they are done.

YIELDS 12 BUNDTS

FOR BUNDTS
6 tablespoons salted butter, softened
1 cup granulated sugar
2 large eggs
1 teaspoon vanilla extract
1½ cups all-purpose flour
½ teaspoon baking powder
½ teaspoon baking soda
1 teaspoon salt
1 tablespoon poppy seeds
¼ cup fresh lemon juice
Zest of 1 lemon
2 tablespoons vegetable oil
½ cup sour cream

FOR GLAZE
2 cups confectioners' sugar
4 tablespoons fresh lemon juice

1. To make Bundts: Preheat oven to 350°F. Grease a mini Bundt pan with nonstick cooking spray and set aside.
2. Cream together butter, sugar, eggs, and vanilla in a stand mixer fitted with paddle attachment until combined, about 1 minute. Add remaining ingredients and mix 2 minutes. Distribute batter evenly among Bundt divots until each is about ¾ full.
3. Bake 20–25 minutes until a knife or toothpick inserted in center comes out clean and tops are brown. Allow to cool in pan 10 minutes, then remove Bundts to a wire rack to cool completely, 1 hour.
4. To make Glaze: Mix sugar and lemon juice together in a medium bowl.
5. Invert each Bundt and dip into Glaze. Allow Glaze to harden onto Bundts, about 10 minutes, before serving.

 **COOKING TIP**

A great idea is to make these the night before you want to eat or serve them and put them in a sealable bag in the refrigerator overnight. Simply allow them to come to room temperature on the counter about an hour before eating!

BEIGNETS

French Street Bistro, Universal Studios Hollywood

....

Most Americans think of beignets as the quintessential New Orleans food, but did you know that Europeans, specifically the French, have been eating beignets since the sixteenth century? Be sure to serve them quickly after they come out of the fryer: They are best hot, fresh, and buried in confectioners' sugar!

SERVES 10

1½ cups warm (110°F) water
½ cup granulated sugar
1 (0.25-ounce) packet active dry yeast
2 large eggs
1¼ teaspoons salt
1 cup evaporated milk
7 cups bread flour, divided
¼ cup vegetable shortening
6 cups vegetable oil, for frying
3 cups confectioners' sugar

1. In a small bowl, stir together water with sugar and yeast. Let bloom 10 minutes.
2. Crack eggs into the bowl of a stand mixer. Using the whisk attachment, beat eggs 1 minute. Add salt and evaporated milk and mix 1 minute. Add yeast mixture and mix 1 minute.
3. Add 3 cups flour while continuing to mix. Add shortening while mixing. Add remaining 4 cups flour while mixing until thoroughly combined.
4. Switch to dough hook attachment and knead until dough comes together, about 5 minutes.
5. Grease a large bowl with nonstick cooking spray. Transfer dough to prepared bowl. Place plastic wrap greased with nonstick cooking spray over top of bowl and let dough rise 3 hours at room temperature.
6. In a large pot over medium heat, heat vegetable oil to 350°F. Line a baking sheet with paper towels and set aside.
7. Flour a flat surface and roll dough out to ¼" thickness. Cut into 2" squares, for a total of about sixty squares.
8. Carefully slide about six dough squares into hot oil and fry about 1 minute on each side until golden brown. Transfer to paper towel–lined baking sheet. Repeat with remaining dough while maintaining oil temperature at 350°F.
9. Serve about six squares per person in cups or bowls, dusted with confectioners' sugar.

CHAPTER 4

APPETIZERS AND SNACKS

Universal has truly elevated the category of theme park snacks. While the Parks do offer all the usual suspects, like popcorn and turkey legs, they also have more unique selections, like Pizza-Stuffed Pretzels, Beef Empanadas, and Korean Corn Dogs. And these exciting eats are easy to make in your own kitchen!

This chapter is full of the popular snacks offered at Universal Theme Parks. Many are easy to eat on the go, like Who Hash and Papas Rellenas. Others make great appetizers to a main course with family, or to impress friends at a party, like Jerk Shrimp Mac and Cheese and Spanakopita Dip. Try out a bunch for a creative meal of small bites, and discover new favorites to come back to again and again!

SCOTCH EGGS

Leaky Cauldron, Universal Studios Florida

A hard-boiled egg wrapped in sausage, rolled in bread crumbs, and deep-fried: sounds like a wacky concoction! The cooks at Fortnum & Mason department store in London developed this dish in 1738 as a portable snack that travelers could take with them after shopping. Seen as an English staple, it can be purchased in many gas stations across the United Kingdom and is still enjoyed by travelers today. Make up a batch for your own travels!

SERVES 2

FOR APPLE BEET SALAD
1 large beet, peeled and cut into ½" cubes
2 tablespoons olive oil, divided
1 teaspoon salt
½ teaspoon ground black pepper
2 sprigs fresh thyme
1 tablespoon apple cider vinegar
½ teaspoon stone-ground mustard
½ teaspoon prepared horseradish
¼ large Granny Smith apple, peeled and cut into ½" cubes

1. To make Apple Beet Salad: Preheat oven to 375°F.
2. Place beet cubes in an 8" × 8" baking dish and drizzle with 1 tablespoon olive oil and sprinkle with salt and pepper. Place thyme sprigs on top of beets, cover with aluminum foil, and bake 1 hour or until beets are fork-tender.
3. Discard thyme sprigs, scoop beets into a medium bowl, and refrigerate 1 hour.
4. In a small bowl, combine vinegar, mustard, and horseradish. Add remaining 1 tablespoon olive oil and whisk vigorously until combined. Add apple cubes to beet cubes and pour in vinegar mixture. Stir to combine and refrigerate 1 hour more.
5. To make Eggs: Preheat oven to 350°F.
6. In a large pot over medium-high heat, heat oil to 325°F.
7. Put beaten egg in a small bowl and bread crumbs in another small bowl.

(continued on next page)

6 cups vegetable oil, for frying
1 large egg, beaten
½ cup plain bread crumbs
½ pound ground pork sausage
2 large hard-boiled eggs

FOR MUSTARD SAUCE
¼ cup mayonnaise
2 tablespoons stone-ground mustard
1 teaspoon lemon juice

FOR SERVING
2 large leaves green leaf lettuce

8. Divide sausage in half and flatten each half into a disc. Place 1 hard-boiled egg in center of each disc and fold sausage inward to completely envelop egg. Roll each wrapped egg in beaten egg, then roll in bread crumbs until fully coated.

9. Gently lower eggs into heated oil and fry until golden brown, 3–5 minutes.

10. Remove eggs with a slotted spoon to a large ungreased ovenproof dish and bake 10–15 minutes until sausage is cooked through to 160°F. Halve eggs and set aside.

11. To make Mustard Sauce: Stir sauce ingredients together in a small bowl.

12. To serve: Place 1 lettuce leaf onto the center of a serving plate. Pack beet mixture into a ½-cup measuring cup (any leftover can be stored in an airtight container in the refrigerator up to 4 days), invert onto lettuce leaf, and remove measuring cup. Place 2 Scotch Egg halves around ½ of Apple Beet Salad. Place a small bowl of Mustard Sauce on side of plate. Repeat with second plate. Serve immediately.

CLAM CHOWD-ARR

The Frying Dutchman, Universal Studios Florida

This delicious soup hails from The Frying Dutchman in Springfield. Featured in *The Simpsons*, The Frying Dutchman serves an all-you-can-eat buffet, taken advantage of by Homer Simpson. The proprietor, Captain McCallister, has to throw Homer out after he eats all the shrimp and two plastic lobsters! Don't worry, there isn't any plastic in this dish—only a creamy base and succulent ocean clams.

SERVES 8

⅓ cup cold salted butter
⅓ cup all-purpose flour
2 tablespoons vegetable oil
2 large Yukon Gold potatoes, peeled and diced
1 medium white onion, peeled and diced
2 medium stalks celery, trimmed and diced
1 cup clam juice
1½ cups heavy whipping cream
2 (8-ounce) cans chopped clams in juice
1 teaspoon ground thyme
½ teaspoon salt
⅛ teaspoon ground white pepper

1. In a small saucepan over medium heat, melt butter, then mix in flour. Continue to cook, stirring frequently, 5 minutes. Remove from heat and set aside.
2. Heat oil in a large pot over medium heat 30 seconds. Add potatoes, onion, and celery. Cook 10 minutes, or until onion is translucent.
3. Add clam juice, cream, canned clams including juice, thyme, salt, white pepper, and butter mixture to pot. Stir to combine and bring to a boil. Once boiling, reduce heat to a simmer and cook 5 minutes, or until potatoes are soft. Ladle into bowls and serve.
4. Store leftovers in an airtight container in refrigerator up to 3 days.

PIZZA-STUFFED PRETZELS

Carmen's Veranda, Universal Studios Florida

....

With all that has been done with pizza, it's only natural that someone would make it into a pretzel. And it's a good thing they did! Be sure to eat this while piping hot to get that *Instagram*-worthy cheese-pull action when you rip into it. Carmen's Veranda is a play on words referring to the popular samba singer Carmen Miranda, who was at the height of fame during the 1930s into the 1950s. You might recognize her in fruit-filled turbans dancing in films such as *Week-End in Havana* or *Down Argentine Way*.

SERVES 2

2½ cups warm (110°F) water, divided
1½ tablespoons dark molasses
1 (0.25-ounce) packet active dry yeast
3 tablespoons salted butter, softened
4 cups all-purpose flour
½ teaspoon salt
2 cups shredded mozzarella cheese, divided
2 tablespoons baking soda
10 medium slices pepperoni
½ cup marinara sauce

1. Combine 1½ cups water, molasses, and yeast in a small bowl and let bloom 10 minutes until froth forms on top.
2. In the bowl of a stand mixer fitted with a dough hook attachment, cream butter, flour, and salt. Add yeast mixture. Knead mixture in bowl on low speed or by hand 8 minutes or until dough is soft and elastic.
3. Cut dough in half. Slowly and carefully roll and pull each dough half into a 4'-long rope. Use a rolling pin to flatten dough ropes to about 3" wide. Sprinkle each rope with ¾ cup mozzarella cheese down the middle, fold over lengthwise, and pinch to seal in cheese.
4. Create a U shape with one rope by holding up each end, then cross the ends and bring them back down toward your body. Spread ends slightly and pinch ends onto pretzel. Repeat with the second rope. Place each pretzel onto a piece of parchment paper and trim paper close to dough. Allow pretzels to rest 20 minutes.
5. Place a baking sheet upside down on middle rack in oven and preheat to 500°F.

(continued on next page)

6. Pour remaining 1 cup water and baking soda into a small saucepan over medium-high heat and bring to a boil. Once boiling, remove from heat. Brush water generously onto pretzels. Place 5 pepperoni slices on each pretzel and sprinkle with remaining ½ cup cheese.
7. Carefully slide one pretzel with parchment paper onto preheated pan in oven. Bake 10–15 minutes until deep brown. Remove from oven and repeat with remaining pretzel. Serve immediately with marinara on the side for dipping.

KOREAN BEEF TACOS

Bumblebee Man's Taco Truck, Universal Studios Florida

Tacos are not originally Korean, but the contents of these tortillas are Korean through and through. Sweet steak pieces and Zesty Cucumber and Radish Topping finished off with fresh lettuce make for a yummy bite. These are a seasonal treat at Bumblebee Man's Taco Truck at the Park, and now you can get a taste of Springfield right at home! The radishes can be cut into thin sticks to match servings offered in the Park.

SERVES 6

FOR ZESTY CUCUMBER AND RADISH TOPPING
½ medium cucumber, peeled and diced
5 radishes, thinly sliced
1 tablespoon finely chopped fresh cilantro
1 teaspoon minced garlic
1 tablespoon soy sauce
2 teaspoons rice vinegar
½ teaspoon sesame oil

FOR KOREAN STEAK
2 tablespoons soy sauce
1 tablespoon light brown sugar
1 tablespoon sesame oil
1 tablespoon minced garlic
1 teaspoon fresh grated ginger
3 (1.5-ounce) flank steaks, sliced into ¼"-thick strips
1 tablespoon vegetable oil

1. To make Zesty Cucumber and Radish Topping: Combine all ingredients in a medium bowl. Allow to marinate in refrigerator 15 minutes up to overnight.
2. To make Korean Steak: In a medium bowl, combine soy sauce, brown sugar, sesame oil, garlic, and ginger. Add steak and toss to coat with marinade, cover, and refrigerate. Allow to marinate 2 hours up to overnight.
3. Heat vegetable oil in a medium pan over medium-high heat. Add steak in a single layer and cook 2–3 minutes, flip, and cook 2–3 minutes more until cooked through to 135°F. Remove to a plate and set aside.

(continued on next page)

FOR ASSEMBLY
6 (4") flour tortillas
1½ cups frisée lettuce
3 cups tortilla chips

4. To Assemble: Place a ¼-cup scoop of Korean Steak into 1 tortilla, add 1–2 tablespoons Zesty Cucumber and Radish Topping, and top with ¼ cup frisée lettuce. Repeat with remaining tortillas, Korean Steak, Zesty Cucumber and Radish Topping, and lettuce. Serve immediately with tortilla chips on the side.

 **MIX IT UP**

At Bumblebee Man's Taco Truck at Universal Studios Florida, you can mix and match tacos to get a taste of more than one kind. Try making the Carne Asada Tacos from this chapter on the same night as these Korean Beef Tacos and enjoy the authentic mix-and-match experience!

SMOKED BRISKET CREPES

Central Park Crêpes, Universal Studios Florida

....

New York is known for a lot of things, not least of which is its street and park food carts. Wanting to replicate the vibe of those carts, Universal built Central Park Crêpes, and people have gone wild for it ever since it opened. Expect to wait in a *long* line if you want a Smoked Brisket Crepe at the Park....Or you could make these at home in a jiffy and enjoy them right away!

SERVES 6

FOR CREPES
1 cup all-purpose flour
2 cups whole milk
4 large egg whites
1 tablespoon vegetable oil
1 tablespoon pure honey
½ teaspoon salt

FOR ASSEMBLY
3 tablespoons ranch dressing
3 tablespoons barbecue sauce
3 cups shredded pepper jack cheese
6 cups precooked sliced brisket
3 cups prepared coleslaw

1. To make Crepes: Add all ingredients to a blender and blend until well combined, about 30 seconds.
2. Heat a large nonstick frying pan over medium heat 30 seconds. Coat pan with nonstick cooking spray. Pour about ¼ cup batter from blender into center of pan, swirling pan while pouring, to fill pan with a thin layer of batter.
3. Allow to cook 1–2 minutes. Once the edges are brown and pulling away from the sides, slide a rubber spatula around entire edge of batter, slip spatula under Crepe, and flip. Cook an additional 1–2 minutes on the other side until no longer wet. Remove to a large plate.
4. Repeat with remaining batter, spraying pan with nonstick cooking spray between each Crepe.
5. To Assemble: In a small bowl, mix together ranch dressing and barbecue sauce.
6. Lay out a still-hot Crepe and sprinkle with ½ cup cheese, 1 cup brisket, and ½ cup coleslaw. Drizzle ⅙ of ranch mixture over toppings. Fold in half, then in half again. Repeat with remaining Crepes and ingredients and serve immediately.

CARNE ASADA TACOS

Bumblebee Man's Taco Truck, Universal Studios Florida

Bumblebee Man doesn't actually sell tacos in The Simpsons' universe; he is an actor! Starring in a Mexican sitcom on "Channel Ocho," he is best known for his slapstick comedy and wacky bee costume. These tacos are a yummy and filling dinner at home. Serve with a side of tortilla chips to complete the meal!

SERVES 6

FOR SALSA
2 (10-ounce) cans diced tomatoes and green chilies, including juice
1 (28-ounce) can whole tomatoes, including juice
⅓ cup chopped fresh cilantro
1 small red onion, peeled and diced
1 teaspoon minced garlic
¼ teaspoon ground cumin
¼ teaspoon salt
¼ teaspoon granulated sugar
2 tablespoons lime juice

FOR CARNE ASADA
3 (1.5-ounce) thin-cut flank steaks
3 teaspoons salt
1½ teaspoons ground black pepper
1 tablespoon vegetable oil

FOR ASSEMBLY
6 (4") flour tortillas
1½ cups shredded sharp Cheddar cheese
1½ cups shredded iceberg lettuce

1. To make Salsa: Add all ingredients to a large blender or food processor and blend until smooth, about 20 seconds. Cover in an airtight container and refrigerate 1 hour. Salsa can be stored in sealed container in refrigerator up to 1 week.
2. To make Carne Asada: Season flank steaks with salt and pepper on both sides. Pour oil into a large skillet over medium-high heat. Add steak and sear 2–4 minutes per side until cooked through to 135°F.
3. Remove steak from skillet to a cutting board and allow to rest 5 minutes. Cut against the grain into ¼" slices.
4. To Assemble: Scoop ¼ cup Carne Asada into 1 flour tortilla. Top with ¼ cup cheese and ¼ cup lettuce. Drizzle on 1 tablespoon Salsa. Repeat with remaining tortillas. Serve immediately.

 **COOKING TIP**

If you want to make these tacos for a crowd, simply multiply the ingredients and make ahead of time. When you're ready to serve, put all the ingredients out for guests to fill the tortillas themselves.

FINNEGAN'S POTATO AND ONION WEBBS

Finnegan's Bar & Grill, Universal Studios Florida

....

An awesome mash-up between fries and onion straws, this crispy, crunchy appetizer has guests at Finnegan's calling the server for another order. Finnegan's is reminiscent of an Irish pub, and nothing says Irish pub like a basket of potato. Luckily this recipe makes *two* Webbs! Finnegan's serves this dish with malt vinegar, but you can serve it with whatever dipping mixture you prefer. Try a campfire-style sauce, with equal parts mayonnaise and barbecue sauce.

SERVES 4

6 cups vegetable oil, for frying
1 cup all-purpose flour
½ cup cornstarch
2 teaspoons garlic powder
1 teaspoon paprika
2 teaspoons salt
1 teaspoon ground black pepper
1 large egg, beaten
¾ cup Guinness Draught beer
½ large yellow onion, peeled and thinly sliced
3 medium russet potatoes, peeled and shredded

1. Pour oil into a large pot and heat to 350°F over medium-high heat. Line a large plate with paper towels and set aside.
2. Mix together flour, cornstarch, garlic powder, paprika, salt, and pepper in a large bowl. Add egg and beer and mix to combine. Add onion and potatoes and gently fold to coat.
3. Carefully scoop ½ of onion and potato mixture into hot oil, gently swirling while adding to break up clumps. Stir and flip continuously 1–3 minutes until golden brown and cooked through. Remove to paper towel–lined plate, confirm oil temperature is maintaining at 350°F, and repeat with remaining mixture. Serve immediately.

WHO HASH

Green Eggs and Ham Cafe, Islands of Adventure

That original Christmas hater himself, the Grinch, raided the residents of *Who*-ville's homes and stole all their presents from under their trees. To add insult to injury, he decided to ransack their pantries and fridges as well, taking every can of *Who*-hash. Universal drew inspiration from this classic Dr. Seuss tale and brought this canned good to life. It's served in an actual tin can, and guests can dip into this strangely delicious meal while visiting Islands of Adventure. If you want to serve your Who Hash in a can, check online for a free printable "Who Hash" label to attach to a cleaned and dull-edged soup can.

SERVES 1

- 2 tablespoons salted butter
- ½ small yellow onion, peeled and diced
- 12 cooked Tater Tots, divided
- 6 ounces cooked and cubed corned beef
- 2 tablespoons white queso, warmed
- 1 tablespoon chopped scallions

1. In a medium pan over medium heat, melt butter, about 1 minute. Add onion and cook 1 minute. Add 8 Tater Tots and cook 5 minutes. Add corned beef and cook 2 minutes.
2. Remove from heat and drizzle on queso.
3. Scoop mixture into a cleaned tin can or cup. Top with remaining 4 Tater Tots and scallions. Serve.

UNIVERSAL PARKS TIP

During the holiday season at Universal, special shows and character meet and greets become available that aren't around the rest of the year. If you're there during November or December, try to slot in some time to visit the Grinch himself. Be careful, though: He is known to insult guests!

SPANAKOPITA DIP

Mythos Restaurant, Islands of Adventure

....

Traditional spanakopita can trace its history back to Greece and is thought to have been around over four hundred years. This works well for Mythos, a restaurant themed to Greek myths and the Greek stories of old. The light fixtures in the bathrooms are in the image of Medusa—don't look too closely! You can also use frozen or canned spinach for this recipe in place of the fresh leaves. The dish will just be a fun green color!

SERVES 2

1 cup plain whole-milk Greek yogurt
1 teaspoon minced garlic
1 cup crumbled feta cheese
1½ cups fresh spinach leaves
1 tablespoon olive oil
1 tablespoon Greek seasoning
2 tablespoons diced Roma tomato
2 tablespoons diced red onion
4 cups pita chips

1. Add Greek yogurt, garlic, and feta cheese to a blender. Pulse five times to mix. Add spinach, olive oil, and Greek seasoning and pulse until spinach is well chopped and incorporated, about 1 minute. Scoop into a medium airtight container and chill in refrigerator at least 1 hour, up to 4 hours.
2. To serve, scoop dip into two bowls and make a divot in the middle of each. Add 1 tablespoon Roma tomato and red onion to each divot and serve with pita chips.

HUMMUS

Doc Sugrue's Desert Kebab House, Islands of Adventure

....

Whether wandering around The Lost Continent or going through your day, an empty stomach is the last thing you need. Fill up with a bowl of hummus, or bring it along with you! This creamy and delicious dip goes great with pita bread, tortilla chips, or raw vegetables. The Lost Continent is an original land in Islands of Adventure that is not tied to a specific Universal movie property. Right next to Doc Sugrue's is a bubbling fountain—that actually talks to passersby!

YIELDS 2 CUPS HUMMUS

1 (15.5-ounce) can garbanzo beans
⅓ cup tahini
¼ cup lemon juice
1 teaspoon salt
2 teaspoons garlic powder
1 tablespoon olive oil
¼ teaspoon paprika

Place all ingredients except paprika in a blender and blend until smooth, about 1 minute. Scoop into a medium bowl and smooth out top. Sprinkle on paprika and serve. Leftovers can be stored in an airtight container in refrigerator up to 1 week.

PULLED PORK NACHOS

The Watering Hole, Islands of Adventure

This is a quick but hearty snack that packs a pork-protein punch (perfect for dinosaur keepers and those who prefer to keep a safe distance, alike), with a freshness lent by the salsa. Try using your favorite salsa, whether it's mild or flaming hot, on this dish. Prepared pulled pork can usually be found in the pork section of the grocery store, and sometimes in the freezer section.

SERVES 1

2 cups tortilla chips
¼ cup white queso, warmed
¼ cup drained and rinsed canned pinto beans, warmed
¼ cup restaurant-style salsa
¼ cup prepared pulled pork, warmed

In a paper tray or on a large plate, pile up chips and layer with queso, beans, salsa, and pulled pork. Serve immediately.

 **COOKING TIP**

If you don't have access to prepared pulled pork, it is quick and easy to make some in a pressure cooker. Simply add 1 cup of beef broth to the pot with 3 pounds of cubed pork roast. Cook on manual for 40 minutes and allow the pressure to naturally release for 10 minutes. Drain pork and you're done!

PAPAS RELLENAS

Natural Selections, Islands of Adventure

Jurassic Park (and Jurassic World) were built on the fictional island Isla Nublar in the waters near Costa Rica. This explains why the Jurassic Park section of Islands of Adventure is highly influenced by Costa Rican cuisine. Found in Costa Rica (though more commonly in Peru), these little fried pockets of mashed potato filled with a spiced beef mixture are a perfect packable lunch or snack.

YIELDS 6 PAPAS RELLENAS

FOR POTATOES
6 cups peeled and cubed russet potatoes
1 teaspoon salt
½ teaspoon ground black pepper
4 tablespoons salted butter, softened
3 tablespoons sour cream

FOR FILLING
1 tablespoon vegetable oil
¼ cup chopped yellow onion
2 teaspoons minced garlic
½ pound lean ground beef
1 teaspoon salt
1 teaspoon ground cumin
½ teaspoon ground black pepper
2 teaspoons ketchup
2 teaspoons distilled white vinegar

1. To make Potatoes: Place potatoes in a large pot and cover with water. Bring to a boil over medium-high heat, then reduce to medium and simmer until fork-tender, about 15 minutes.
2. Drain potatoes and return to pot. Mash with a potato masher. Add salt, pepper, butter, and sour cream and stir and mash until smooth. Set aside to cool, 30–45 minutes.
3. To make Filling: Heat vegetable oil in a medium skillet over medium heat. Add onion and garlic and cook 5 minutes. Add ground beef and cook until brown and has reached an internal temperature of 160°F, 5–8 minutes.
4. Add salt, cumin, pepper, ketchup, and vinegar to skillet and stir to combine. Allow to simmer until liquids have evaporated, about 5 minutes. Remove from heat to cool, about 30 minutes.
5. To Assemble: Line a baking sheet with plastic wrap and set aside. Crack eggs into a small bowl and beat. Add bread crumbs to another small bowl and flour to a third small bowl.

2 large eggs
1 cup plain bread crumbs
1 cup all-purpose flour
6 cups vegetable oil, for
 frying

6. Once Potatoes and Filling have cooled enough to handle, scoop about 3 tablespoons Potatoes into one hand and use the other hand to create a divot in the middle, about the size of a golf ball. Add 1-2 tablespoons Filling and add more Potatoes to the top to seal. Use your hands to shape the Papa Rellena into a ball or a slight cone. Gently roll in flour, then egg (making sure to massage egg through flour so it coats), and then bread crumbs. Shake off any excess. Place on prepared baking sheet. Repeat with remaining Potatoes and Filling. Refrigerate 2–4 hours until solid and not mushy.

7. To Fry: Pour oil into a large pot and heat over medium heat to 350°F. Line a large plate with paper towels and set aside. Gently lower balls one at a time into oil and fry three or four at a time. Turn frequently until crispy and brown, 3–5 minutes. Remove to paper towel–lined plate, confirm oil is maintained at 350°F, and repeat with remaining balls. Allow to cool slightly, then serve.

BEEF EMPANADAS

Natural Selections, Islands of Adventure

These satisfying empanadas are loaded with beefy filling (though you can swap in a plant-based option instead if desired!). The name of the food stand where they are served, Natural Selections, has double meaning. While the selections here are made from natural ingredients, the name also alludes to the term "natural selection," which was popularized by Charles Darwin in his studies of how animal species adapt over time. This idea is played out repeatedly in the Jurassic Park franchise as scientists *unnaturally* push the limit in creating more and more dangerous dinos.

YIELDS 8 EMPANADAS

1 (2-count) box refrigerated pie crusts
½ pound beef cube steak, chopped
1 teaspoon salt
½ teaspoon ground black pepper
1 teaspoon vegetable oil
½ cup diced yellow onion
2.5 ounces ground chorizo
1 teaspoon garlic powder
1 teaspoon dried thyme leaves
1 teaspoon ground marjoram
1 tablespoon tomato paste
2 teaspoons paprika

1. Allow pie crusts to come to room temperature, about 45 minutes.
2. Meanwhile, prepare filling. Season beef with salt and pepper on all sides. Heat oil in a large skillet over medium-high heat, about 2 minutes. Add beef and cook until browned, about 5 minutes.
3. Reduce heat to medium and add onion and chorizo and cook 10 minutes. Add garlic powder, thyme, marjoram, tomato paste, and paprika. Stir until liquids evaporate, about 10 minutes.
4. Preheat oven to 375°F. Line a baking sheet with parchment paper and set aside. Unroll both pie crusts onto a lightly floured surface. Using a 4" circular pot or container lid as a guide, cut out 4" circles, about four from each crust. Run a moistened finger along the outer rim of each circle. Scoop 2–3 tablespoons beef filling into each circle (you can eat or discard any excess filling), fold circles in half, and press edges together with fingers to seal.
5. Bake empanadas on prepared baking sheet 10–15 minutes until golden brown. Serve immediately.

TURKEY LEGS

Thunder Falls Terrace, Islands of Adventure

Out of all the dishes served across America's theme parks, the turkey leg may be *the* quintessential theme park food. It's hearty, it's portable, it's delicious, and it's big enough to share (if that's your thing). Plus it looks like something a T. rex would devour. Serve with a side of fries for a meal.

SERVES 2

2 tablespoons salt
2 tablespoons light brown
   sugar
1 cup water
2 (12-ounce) turkey
   drumsticks

1. Combine salt, brown sugar, and water in a large plastic zip-top bag. Add turkey drumsticks and allow to brine in refrigerator 24 hours.
2. Preheat oven to 350°F.
3. Place a wire rack on top of a baking sheet. Remove drumsticks from bag and place on wire rack. Bake until internal temperature reaches 165°F, about 1 hour, 15 minutes.
4. Allow to cool 10 minutes on rack, then serve.

JERK SHRIMP MAC AND CHEESE

Whakawaiwai Eats, Volcano Bay

....

Jerk cooking and seasoning are native to the Caribbean and involve bright spices rubbed into meats that are then grilled or pan cooked. This dish was created to bring the flavors of the islands to Volcano Bay, while still offering the beloved American comfort food of mac and cheese. The two work together quite nicely! Feel free to add more cayenne pepper to the dish if you prefer your jerk with a little more kick.

SERVES 1

FOR JERK SEASONING
1 tablespoon dried minced onion
1 teaspoon dried thyme leaves
1 teaspoon ground allspice
1 teaspoon ground black pepper
¼ teaspoon ground cinnamon
¼ teaspoon ground cayenne
  pepper
½ teaspoon salt

FOR WHITE CHEDDAR CHEESE SAUCE
1½ tablespoons salted butter
1½ tablespoons all-purpose flour
¾ cup whole milk
½ teaspoon salt
1 cup grated white Cheddar
  cheese

FOR MAC AND CHEESE
2 cups cooked elbow macaroni
  noodles, warmed
5 uncooked jumbo shrimp,
  peeled and deveined, tails on
3 tablespoons vegetable oil,
  divided
1 teaspoon chopped fresh
  cilantro

1. To make Jerk Seasoning: In a small bowl or container, mix together all ingredients. Set aside.
2. To make White Cheddar Cheese Sauce: In a medium saucepan over medium heat, melt butter. Whisk in flour until smooth, about 1 minute. Add milk, reduce heat to low, and simmer 1 minute. Stir in ½ teaspoon prepared Jerk Seasoning and salt. Add cheese and stir until melted and smooth, about 2 minutes.
3. To Assemble Mac and Cheese: Pour White Cheddar Cheese Sauce over noodles in a medium bowl and toss to combine.
4. In a separate medium bowl, toss shrimp in 2 tablespoons vegetable oil and cover in remaining Jerk Seasoning. Heat remaining 1 tablespoon oil in a clean medium saucepan over medium-high heat. Add shrimp and cook 3–4 minutes per side until cooked through.
5. Place shrimp on top of macaroni, garnish with cilantro, and serve immediately.

ISLAND CHICKEN SALAD

Whakawaiwai Eats, Volcano Bay

....

If you haven't yet been to Volcano Bay, you should give it a try next time you're in central Florida. Touted as a water theme park, Volcano Bay boasts immersive theming and incredible water rides that meet you around every corner. But the most markedly different aspect of the Park is the overarching feel of tropical vibes and beachy scenes. And the food is no exception. Dishes like this Island Chicken Salad are fresh, fruity, and fun and make you feel like you're eating in paradise. Try it at home for a respite any day. Add even more fruity flavor with sliced pineapple and strawberries!

SERVES 1

FOR DRESSING
½ cup cream of coconut
¼ cup pineapple juice
¼ cup lime juice
1 teaspoon dried cilantro
½ teaspoon garlic powder
½ teaspoon salt

FOR SALAD
2 cups diced cooked chicken
1 cup halved red grapes
1 cup diced Fuji apple
2 tablespoons sliced almonds

1. To make Dressing: Combine all ingredients in a small bowl. Set aside.
2. To make Salad: Toss together chicken, grapes, and apples in a medium bowl. Drizzle on desired amount of Dressing and sprinkle with sliced almonds. Store leftover Dressing in an airtight container in refrigerator up to 1 week.

VEGETARIAN CORN DOGS

Mummy Eats, Universal Studios Hollywood

Here we have a classic corn dog—without the hot dog! Plant-based "hot dogs" are easy to find and can be purchased at most grocery or big-box stores. If you'd like to turn your Vegetarian Corn Dog into a Korean Vegetarian Corn Dog, just follow the recipe in this chapter for Korean Corn Dogs but sub in a plant-based dog instead! They're made to take on the go after you brave Revenge of the Mummy–The Ride in the Park, but you can serve these with a side of fries for a filling meal at home.

SERVES 6

6 cups vegetable oil, for frying
1 cup yellow cornmeal
1 cup all-purpose flour
½ cup granulated sugar
½ teaspoon salt
½ teaspoon ground black pepper
4 teaspoons baking powder
1½ cups whole milk
1 large egg
6 plant-based hot dogs

1. In a large pot over medium heat, heat vegetable oil to 350°F. Line a large plate with paper towels and set aside.
2. In a medium bowl, mix together cornmeal, flour, sugar, salt, pepper, and baking powder. Add milk and egg, then whisk.
3. Pour batter into a tall drinking glass ¾ full (if it doesn't all fit, refill glass when necessary). Insert one wooden chopstick or ice pop stick into each hot dog and dry each hot dog with a paper towel to help batter stick. Dip 1 hot dog into batter in glass.
4. Carefully lower coated hot dog immediately into hot oil. Repeat coating and frying with up to 3 dogs at a time. Fry until golden brown, about 3 minutes, turning frequently.
5. Transfer to paper towel–lined plate. Serve immediately.

GRILLED ELOTE WITH TAJÍN

Little Cocina, Universal Studios Hollywood

....

During the fall, Universal Studios Hollywood and Universal Studios Florida host their largest event of the year: Halloween Horror Nights. This Parks-wide event includes fully immersive haunted houses, live entertainment, free-roaming scare actors, and—of course—delicious culinary offerings! This dish is one such offering that can only be obtained at Universal during Halloween Horror Nights; now you can enjoy it any time of year. Delicious grilled corn on the cob is slathered in lime butter and sprinkled with spicy Tajín.

SERVES 6

6 ears corn, with husks
   pulled back
½ cup salted butter, softened
2 teaspoons lime juice
6 teaspoons Tajín seasoning
6 wedges key lime

1. Heat an outdoor grill or a grill pan on the stove to medium-high heat (if using a grill pan, rub pan with 1 tablespoon vegetable oil). Add corn and cook, turning frequently, 10 minutes, or until bright yellow and slightly charred. Remove from heat to six plates.
2. Stir together butter and lime juice in a small bowl. Slather generously over corn. Sprinkle with Tajín. Enjoy immediately with lime wedges for spritzing.

UNIVERSAL PARKS TIP

Halloween Horror Nights are not for the faint of heart. They're recommended for mature audiences thirteen and older, so be prepared for guts and gore like you've never seen before. Most of the haunted houses are themed to classic and modern horror movies, but Universal also throws in original IP, like Revenge of the Tooth Fairy.

KOREAN CORN DOGS

Mummy Eats, Universal Studios Hollywood

How is a Korean Corn Dog different from your typical American corn dog?
There are a couple of key differences: First, it is rolled in panko. This gives the
corn dog a special crunch, unlike smooth corn dogs. Second, there is a sprinkling
of sugar at the end. If you sprinkle sugar onto a corn dog while it is still hot, the
sugar melts into the crust, offering sweet notes to the corn batter. Mummy Eats
serves this mouthwatering treat so that hungry guests can munch on a delicious
handheld snack after braving Revenge of the Mummy–The Ride.
Serve with a side of fries at home for a full meal.

SERVES 6

6 cups vegetable oil,
   for frying
1¼ cups all-purpose flour
2 tablespoons plus 6
   teaspoons granulated
   sugar, divided
½ teaspoon salt
2 teaspoons baking powder
½ cup whole milk
1 large egg
1 cup panko bread crumbs
6 beef hot dogs

1. Pour oil into a large pot over medium heat and bring
   to 350°F. Line a large plate with paper towels and
   set aside.
2. Meanwhile, combine flour, 2 tablespoons sugar, salt,
   baking powder, milk, and egg in a medium bowl. Pour
   batter into a tall drinking glass ¾ full (if it doesn't all fit,
   refill glass when necessary). Pour panko into a shallow
   dish.
3. Skewer each hot dog with a wooden chopstick or ice
   pop stick. Dry each hot dog with a paper towel. Dunk
   skewered hot dogs, one at a time, in glass of batter,
   then roll in panko.
4. Carefully lower battered hot dogs into hot oil (only fry
   1 or 2 at a time to avoid dropping oil temperature) and
   fry 2–3 minutes until golden brown. Repeat for all
5. hot dogs.
6. Remove from oil onto paper towel–lined plate and
   sprinkle each corn dog with 1 teaspoon sugar.
   Serve immediately.

CHAPTER 5

ENTRÉES

Now we are getting into the meat and potatoes of this book—or should we say, the Cottage Pie and Chicken Thumbs? Either way, with a wide variety of delicious main dishes offered at Universal Parks, there are new favorites waiting to be discovered.

Many of the dishes and locations in this chapter may be recognized from popular Universal Parks properties, like the Krusty Burger from The Simpsons and a sampling of the filling meals from Three Broomsticks, featured in Harry Potter. But you may also find dishes you haven't yet heard of, including tropical wonders like Jerked Mahi Sandwiches from Volcano Bay, or inventive recipes like Fork, Knife, and Spoon Grilled Cheese from Universal's signature table-service restaurant, Mythos. And the creatively tasty takes inspired by Jurassic Park are sure to please the whole family. Making the foods you've craved from fiction, as well as trying out new flavors, will bring excitement to your home at mealtime.

FISHERMAN'S PIE

Leaky Cauldron, Universal Studios Florida

The Leaky Cauldron in the Harry Potter franchise is known to wizards and witches for serving delicious comfort foods. And thanks to Universal Parks, muggles can partake as well. This dish is a cross between chicken potpie and shepherd's pie but with a seafood twist. You can use frozen fish fillets as they are easy and inexpensive, or you can use fresh fish.

SERVES 6

3 medium russet potatoes, peeled and cubed
1¾ cups whole milk, divided
4 tablespoons salted butter, divided
4 teaspoons salt, divided
3 teaspoons ground black pepper, divided
½ cup all-purpose flour
1 (6-ounce) fillet salmon, cubed
1 (6-ounce) fillet cod, cubed
4 ounces medium cooked tail-off shrimp, halved
1 tablespoon Dijon mustard
1 tablespoon chopped fresh chives
2 teaspoons garlic powder
⅓ cup drained canned corn
⅓ cup frozen peas

1. Preheat oven to 400°F. Grease six medium ramekins with nonstick cooking spray and set aside.
2. Boil potatoes in a medium pot of water over medium-high heat until fork-tender, 15–20 minutes. Remove from heat and drain.
3. Add ¼ cup milk and 2 tablespoons butter to pot and smash with a potato masher until smooth. Add 2 teaspoons salt and 2 teaspoons pepper and stir well. Set aside.
4. In a medium saucepan over medium heat, add remaining 2 tablespoons butter and flour and stir well. Cook 1–2 minutes until golden brown. Gradually whisk in remaining 1½ cups milk and cook 3–4 minutes more until warmed.
5. Remove flour mixture from heat and add in salmon, cod, shrimp, mustard, remaining 2 teaspoons salt, remaining 1 teaspoon pepper, chives, garlic powder, corn, and peas. Divide among ramekins. Spoon potatoes on top and smooth over fish mixture.
6. Carefully place ramekins into oven and bake 20–25 minutes until filling is hot and bubbling. Allow to cool slightly, about 10 minutes, before serving.

COTTAGE PIE

Leaky Cauldron, Universal Studios Florida

The Leaky Cauldron is the first magical establishment that Harry Potter ever encounters in the franchise. It becomes a place of security and comfort for him throughout the book and movie series. Cottage Pie is the perfect comfort food—a warm meal that is easy to whip up and get on the table. If you don't eat beef, try substituting Impossible or Beyond plant-based burger for a meatless meal! Pair your pie with a side salad.

SERVES 6

3 medium russet potatoes, peeled and cubed
¼ cup whole milk
2 tablespoons salted butter
3 teaspoons salt, divided
3 teaspoons ground black pepper, divided
1 tablespoon vegetable oil
1 pound lean ground beef
1 medium yellow onion, peeled and diced
¾ cup diced carrot
2 tablespoons all-purpose flour
½ teaspoon ground cinnamon
1 tablespoon Italian seasoning
2 tablespoons chopped fresh parsley
1½ cups beef broth
1 tablespoon tomato paste

1. Preheat oven to 400°F. Grease six medium ramekins with nonstick cooking spray and set aside.
2. Boil potatoes in a medium pot of water over medium-high heat until fork-tender, about 15–20 minutes. Remove from heat and drain.
3. Add milk and butter to potatoes and smash with a potato masher until smooth. Add 2 teaspoons salt and 2 teaspoons pepper and stir well. Set aside.
4. Heat oil in a large skillet over medium heat. Add ground beef, remaining 1 teaspoon salt, and remaining 1 teaspoon pepper and cook while stirring frequently for 3 minutes. Add onion and carrot and cook until meat is browned through, 8–9 minutes. Add in flour, cinnamon, Italian seasoning, and parsley and cook 2 minutes more.
5. Add in beef broth and tomato paste and reduce heat to medium-low. Simmer 15 minutes or until most of the liquid has been evaporated.
6. Spoon meat mix into prepared ramekins and smooth mashed potatoes over top of each. Bake 20–25 minutes until filling is bubbly and hot. Serve immediately.

BEEF, LAMB, AND GUINNESS STEW

Leaky Cauldron, Universal Studios Florida

The Leaky Cauldron is a wizard establishment in the Harry Potter books where witches and wizards can order a hot meal before embarking through an enchanted brick wall into the whimsical shopping district that is Diagon Alley. Beef, Lamb, and Guinness Stew is exactly the sort of thing that would be ladled up from a huge cast-iron cauldron into a bread bowl.

SERVES 6

1½ pounds lamb shoulder, cubed

1½ pounds beef roast, cubed

1 teaspoon salt

1 teaspoon ground black pepper

3 tablespoons olive oil

1 medium yellow onion, peeled and diced

2 teaspoons minced garlic

2 tablespoons plus ¾ cup water, divided

1 tablespoon tomato paste

2 tablespoons all-purpose flour

½ cup Guinness Draught beer

1½ cups beef broth

1 bay leaf

1 sprig fresh rosemary

1 teaspoon granulated sugar

2 large carrots, peeled and diced

2 cups quartered baby potatoes

⅓ cup frozen peas

⅓ cup heavy whipping cream

6 Italian bread bowls (optional)

1. Sprinkle lamb and beef with salt and pepper. Heat oil in a large pot over medium-high heat and add lamb. Cook lamb and beef, in batches if needed, until outsides are browned, 5–8 minutes. Remove meat from pot and set aside.

2. Into same pot, add onion, garlic, and 2 tablespoons water. Cook, stirring and scraping, until onion is soft, about 5 minutes. Add tomato paste and cook 2 minutes more.

3. Add lamb and beef cubes back into pot and add flour. Stir until combined and cook 1–2 minutes. Add in beer, beef broth, remaining ¾ cup water, bay leaf, rosemary, and sugar. Stir and cover, then reduce heat to low and simmer 45 minutes.

4. Add in carrots and potatoes and simmer uncovered an additional 30–45 minutes until vegetables are fork-tender.

5. Remove bay leaf and rosemary sprig and add in peas. Cook 3 minutes until peas are thawed and warmed. Add in cream and stir until well combined.

6. Ladle stew into bread bowls (or soup bowls if not using bread bowls) and serve immediately. Leftovers can be stored in refrigerator in an airtight container up to 5 days.

CHICKEN THUMBS

Cletus' Chicken Shack, Universal Studios Florida

Although you might question what's being battered and fried at the fictional Cletus' Chicken Shack in Springfield, you can be 100 percent confident that what you're making at home is fresh boneless, skinless chicken breast and has *no* thumbs in it whatsoever. Make them a full meal by pairing with crinkle-cut fries or Tater Tots (Universal serves with fries) and coleslaw.

SERVES 6

6 cups vegetable oil, for frying
1½ cups all-purpose flour
1 teaspoon salt
1 teaspoon ground black pepper
1 teaspoon onion powder
1 teaspoon garlic powder
1 large egg
1 tablespoon water
1½ pounds boneless, skinless chicken breasts, cut into 1"-thick strips

1. In a large pot over medium heat, bring oil to 340°F.
2. Meanwhile, in a medium shallow bowl, stir together flour, salt, pepper, onion powder, and garlic powder. In a separate shallow bowl, beat together egg and water.
3. Dredge each chicken strip in flour mixture, then egg mixture, then flour mixture again. Place on a large plate and allow to rest 5 minutes.
4. Line a separate large plate with paper towels and set aside.
5. Carefully lower 5 strips into hot oil one at a time and allow to fry until internal temperature is 165°F, about 8 minutes. Remove from oil onto paper towel–lined plate. Repeat with remaining strips. Serve immediately.

CHICKEN AND WAFFLE SANDWICHES

Cletus' Chicken Shack, Universal Studios Florida

Whoever came up with the chicken and waffle idea deserves an award:
It's genius! Crispy, savory chicken with thick, slightly sweet waffles is a
winning combination for sure. Universal has made it even easier
to make at home by using frozen waffles.

SERVES 6

½ cup mayonnaise
2 tablespoons pure maple
  syrup
1 tablespoon light brown
  sugar
12 Belgian-style frozen
  waffles, toasted
12 Chicken Thumbs (see
  recipe in this chapter)
6 pieces iceberg lettuce
12 slices beefsteak tomato
1 cup prepared Tater Tots

1. Combine mayonnaise, maple syrup, and brown sugar in
   a small bowl. Lay out toasted waffles and spread
   1 tablespoon sauce each onto 6 waffles.
2. Onto sauce on each waffle, lay 2 Chicken Thumbs
   followed by 1 piece lettuce, 2 tomato slices, and another
   waffle. Skewer each sandwich with a large toothpick
   and serve with Tater Tots.

SIMPLIFICATION HACK

*If you want to make this meal even easier to get on the table, use frozen
chicken fingers (heated following package instructions) instead of the
homemade Chicken Thumbs.*

MYTHOS SIGNATURE LAMB BURGERS

Mythos Restaurant, Islands of Adventure

....

This burger is nothing like one from a local diner. It uses ingredients common in Mediterranean dishes, making it a perfect fit for the Mythos lineup. Ground lamb has a similar texture to ground beef, but it has a deeper, somewhat gamy, flavor. The sumptuous Feta and Olive Aioli levels up this burger much more than ketchup or mustard could. Make some fries and dip them in the aioli too!

SERVES 4

FOR FETA AND OLIVE AIOLI
- ¼ cup pitted, diced kalamata olives
- ½ cup crumbled feta cheese
- 3 tablespoons mayonnaise
- 4 tablespoons plain whole-milk Greek yogurt
- ¼ teaspoon ground black pepper
- 1 teaspoon minced garlic

FOR LAMB BURGERS
- 1 pound ground lamb
- 2 tablespoons dried minced onion
- 1 teaspoon garlic powder
- 1 tablespoon dried parsley
- 1 teaspoon dried oregano
- 1 teaspoon ground cumin
- ¼ teaspoon paprika
- 1 teaspoon salt
- ½ teaspoon ground black pepper
- 2 tablespoons olive oil, divided
- 4 slices red onion

1. To make Feta and Olive Aioli: Add all ingredients to a blender or food processor and pulse until combined and smooth, about 1 minute. Set aside.
2. To make Lamb Burgers: Preheat a grill or grill pan to medium heat.
3. Add ground lamb, minced onion, garlic powder, parsley, oregano, cumin, paprika, salt, and pepper to a medium bowl. Mix well until fully combined. Divide into four balls.
4. Grease grill or grill pan with 1 tablespoon olive oil and add balls of mixture to grill or grill pan, flattening each ball with a spatula. Cook 3–5 minutes on each side until inserted thermometer reads 160°F. Remove patties to a plate.
5. Add 1 tablespoon more olive oil to grill or pan and cook red onion slices slightly, 2 minutes per side. Remove from heat to plate with patties.

FOR ASSEMBLY
1 tablespoon olive oil
4 brioche burger buns
1 cup shredded iceberg
lettuce
4 slices beefsteak tomato
4 whole pitted kalamata
olives

6. To Assemble: In a clean medium frying pan, heat olive oil over medium heat. Add buns to pan, cut side down, and toast 1–2 minutes until toasted to preference. Remove to plate with patties.
7. Layer each bottom bun with ¼ cup shredded lettuce, 1 tomato slice, 1 Lamb Burger, 1 grilled onion slice, ¼ of Feta and Olive Aioli, and a top bun. Place a toothpick through each top bun and add a kalamata olive to toothpick to finish. Serve.

UNIVERSAL PARKS TIP

Universal Parks has an official podcast called Discover Universal, *with super-informative episodes that include detailed guides of the Parks and Resorts. Give it a listen before your next trip!*

FORK, KNIFE, AND SPOON GRILLED CHEESE

Mythos Restaurant, Islands of Adventure

....

Grilled cheese sandwiches can sometimes be labeled as "basic"; however, this meal is anything but! A mash-up of the classics of grilled cheese, tomato soup, and potato chips combined into one, this phenomenal dish is worthy of the gods honored at Mythos. Next time you dine at Mythos, check out the open kitchen, where you can view chefs chopping and grilling your meal right in front of you!

SERVES 1

FOR TOMATO SOUP
1 tablespoon olive oil
½ large red onion, peeled and diced
½ teaspoon salt
2 teaspoons minced garlic
½ cup white cooking wine
4 medium ripe Roma tomatoes, diced
4 large fresh basil leaves, sliced
1 cup tomato juice

FOR HOMEMADE CHIPS
4 Gemstone or Baby Dutch potatoes, sliced thin
1 tablespoon olive oil

FOR GRILLED CHEESE SANDWICH
1 tablespoon olive oil
2 thick slices white bread

1. To make Tomato Soup: Heat olive oil in a large pot over medium heat. Add onion and salt and cook until soft, 8–9 minutes. Add garlic, stir, and cook 2–3 minutes more.

2. Add wine to pot, stir, and cook 3 minutes. Add tomatoes and stir frequently while cooking 10 minutes. Add basil.

3. Using an immersion blender (or working in batches in a stand blender), purée until smooth. Add tomato juice and stir to combine. Reduce heat to low and simmer 15 minutes.

4. To make Homemade Chips: Soak potato slices in ice water 10 minutes. Remove and dry thoroughly on paper towels, then drizzle with olive oil. Line a large plate with fresh paper towels and set aside.

5. Air fry at 360°F 8–10 minutes, flipping halfway through, until crispy. Remove to paper towel–lined plate.

6. To make Grilled Cheese Sandwich: Heat a large skillet over medium heat. Drizzle olive oil on one side of each bread slice. Place 1 slice on skillet, oil side down.

(continued on next page)

2 tablespoons shredded
  sharp Cheddar cheese
2 tablespoons shredded
  mozzarella cheese
2 tablespoons shredded
  pepper jack cheese

FOR ASSEMBLY
½ teaspoon balsamic vinegar
1 tablespoon bacon bits
1 tablespoon grated
  Parmesan cheese
1 teaspoon chopped fresh
  chives

7. Mix cheeses together in a small bowl, then pile cheese onto bread slice in skillet and top with other bread slice, oil side up. Cook until underside is brown and cheese starts to melt, 2–4 minutes. Flip and continue cooking until cheeses are fully melted and other bread side is browned, 2–3 minutes. Remove from pan and set aside.

8. To Assemble: Ladle about ½ cup Tomato Soup into a medium shallow bowl. Drizzle balsamic vinegar onto soup. Place Grilled Cheese Sandwich on top of soup. Sprinkle with bacon bits, Homemade Chips, Parmesan cheese, and chives. Serve immediately. Leftover Tomato Soup can be stored in an airtight container in refrigerator up to 3 days.

CHICKEN KEBAB

Doc Sugrue's Desert Kebab House, Islands of Adventure

....

The kebab—meat cooked on a stick—dates all the way back to the seventeenth century B.C.E.; archaeologists found stone supports over firepits used to hold skewers of meat. It fits nicely into the theme of "The Lost Continent," where Doc Sugrue's is located at Islands of Adventure. These meat sticks are delicious and make a perfect handheld snack at the Park and at home!

SERVES 1

½ cup plain whole-milk Greek yogurt
2 tablespoons olive oil
2 tablespoons lemon juice
4 teaspoons minced garlic
1 tablespoon dried oregano
1 teaspoon salt
½ teaspoon ground black pepper
1 (4-ounce) boneless, skinless chicken breast, cubed
½ medium red bell pepper, seeded and cubed
½ medium green bell pepper, seeded and cubed
1 (6") piece pita bread
1 tablespoon tzatziki sauce
¼ cup shredded iceberg lettuce
2 tablespoons diced Roma tomato

1. In a small bowl, mix together yogurt, olive oil, lemon juice, garlic, oregano, salt, and black pepper. Add chicken cubes, mix to coat, and allow to marinate 2 hours in refrigerator.
2. Soak a wooden skewer in water 30 minutes. Preheat a grill pan over medium-high heat 3 minutes. Grease pan with nonstick cooking spray.
3. Skewer chicken, red bell pepper, and green bell pepper in a repeating pattern on wooden skewer. Place on grill pan and cook 4 minutes per side, or until internal temperature of chicken reaches 165°F. Remove from heat.
4. Place pita bread on a plate and spread on tzatziki sauce. Sprinkle with lettuce and tomato and lay skewer on top. Serve.

FISH AND CHIPS

Three Broomsticks, Islands of Adventure

The podcast *Very Amusing* with Carlye Wisel delves into the deep questions asked about theme parks. In one episode, she met with chefs and food creators at Universal Parks and asked the pressing question: How are their fish and chips so good? The answer was simple: They use the freshest fish! Every day, fresh-caught Bering Sea cod is flown in directly to Universal Parks and battered and fried right there in the restaurant, never seeing a freezer. Serve with tartar sauce for dipping. While the child's serving at Three Broomsticks includes a side of grapes, the adult serving does not, so feel free to add or leave out as desired.

SERVES 2

½ cup all-purpose flour, divided
½ cup cornstarch
½ cup ginger ale
6 cups vegetable oil, for frying
4 (7-ounce) fresh cod fillets, sliced ½" thick
1 teaspoon salt
½ teaspoon ground black pepper
½ cup cooked wedge fries

1. In a medium bowl, mix together ¼ cup flour, cornstarch, and ginger ale. Refrigerate 30 minutes.
2. Heat oil in a large pot over medium heat to 350°F. Line a large plate with paper towels and set aside.
3. Place remaining ¼ cup flour in a shallow dish. Dry fish pieces thoroughly with a paper towel, then season with salt and pepper on each side. Dredge fish in flour, shake off excess, then dip in chilled batter and allow excess to drip back into bowl.
4. Carefully lower fish into hot oil, frying two pieces at a time. Turning frequently, fry 5–8 minutes until internal temperature reaches 145°F and coating is golden brown.
5. Transfer to paper towel–lined plate and repeat with remaining fish pieces, confirming that oil temperature is maintained at 350°F. Serve immediately with wedge fries on the side.

SPARERIBS PLATTER

Three Broomsticks, Islands of Adventure

You may have never heard of HP Sauce before. "HP" stands for "Houses of Parliament," not "Harry Potter," as you may have thought. Its creation dates to the early 1900s in England, and it has become the most popular brown sauce across the UK. Even British Commonwealth countries, like Canada, love their HP Sauce! HP Sauce can usually be found in the condiment section of any grocery store, but if you're having trouble finding it there, check the imports section where other British goods might be sold.

SERVES 3

FOR RIBS
1 tablespoon salt
2 teaspoons ground white pepper
1 fresh bay leaf, crushed
1 (3½-pound) piece pork loin back ribs
1 cup HP Sauce
⅓ cup ketchup
2 tablespoons brown mustard
2 tablespoons Worcestershire sauce
¾ cup apple juice
¼ cup pure honey

1. To make Ribs: Preheat oven to 275°F. Line a baking sheet with aluminum foil and set aside.
2. Mix together salt, white pepper, and crushed bay leaf in a small bowl. Rub over top and bottom of ribs. Place ribs on prepared baking sheet.
3. Mix together HP sauce, ketchup, mustard, Worcestershire sauce, apple juice, and honey in an 8" × 8" baking dish.
4. Place dish on bottom rack of oven. Place baking sheet of ribs on middle rack of oven. Bake 3 hours. During baking, prepare Roasted Potatoes and Corn on the Cob. In the last hour of baking, spoon ¼ of the sauce from bottom dish over ribs every 15 minutes until bottom dish is empty.
5. Remove dish from oven. Preheat broiler to high and broil ribs on high heat 4 minutes. Remove from oven and allow ribs to rest 5 minutes. Use a sharp knife to cut rack into three pieces. Place on serving plates.

(continued on next page)

4 medium russet potatoes,
  peeled and sliced ¼" thick
4 tablespoons olive oil
2 teaspoons salt
1 teaspoon ground black
  pepper
1 teaspoon garlic powder
2 teaspoons dried rosemary

3 ears corn, with husks
  pulled back
¼ cup salted butter, softened
1 teaspoon salt
½ teaspoon ground black
  pepper

6. To make Roasted Potatoes: Preheat oven to 400°F.
   Grease a baking sheet with nonstick cooking spray and
   set aside.

7. In a large bowl, stir together potato slices, olive oil, salt,
   pepper, garlic powder, and rosemary. Lay potatoes
   on prepared baking sheet in a single layer and bake
   40–50 minutes, turning halfway through cooking time,
   until slightly soft and browned. Remove from oven and
   divide onto serving plates.

8. To make Corn on the Cob: Preheat a grill pan or
   outdoor grill to medium-high heat. If using a grill pan,
   grease with nonstick cooking spray. Add corn and cook,
   turning frequently, 10 minutes, or until bright yellow
   and slightly charred. Remove from heat.

9. Slather butter generously over corn. Sprinkle with salt
   and pepper. Place on serving plates. Serve.

ROASTED PERNIL

Thunder Falls Terrace, Islands of Adventure

Traditionally served in Puerto Rico for special occasions like birthdays, this dish is slow roasted for loved ones. Marked by buttery and tender meat topped with a crispy skin, you may want to make it more often than just the occasional birthday! Sweet plantains offset the rich meat. Serve with rice and black beans.

SERVES 6

FOR PORK
1 (2½-pound) skin-on pork roast
2 tablespoons vegetable oil
3 tablespoons minced garlic
1 tablespoon dried oregano
1 tablespoon adobo seasoning
1 tablespoon paprika
1 teaspoon salt
½ teaspoon ground black pepper
2 tablespoons pulp-free orange juice

FOR SWEET PLANTAINS
½ cup vegetable oil
3 large ripe plantains, peeled and cut into 4 pieces each

1. To make Pork: Preheat oven to 300°F. Place pork roast, skin side up, in a large casserole dish.
2. Mix together oil, garlic, oregano, adobo, paprika, salt, and pepper in a small bowl. Smear all over pork roast.
3. Cover dish with lid or aluminum foil and bake 3 hours. Remove cover and cook an additional 3 hours.
4. Carefully remove from oven and drizzle on orange juice. Remove roast from pan and allow to sit on a cutting board 30 minutes to rest.
5. To make Sweet Plantains: Line a large plate with paper towels. In a medium skillet, heat oil over medium-high heat 5 minutes. Add plantains and fry 2–3 minutes per side until golden. Remove to paper towel–lined plate.
6. Serve Pork sliced or shredded with crispy skin on top on six serving plates, beside Sweet Plantains.

COCONUT-CRUSTED FRIED CHICKEN

Kohola Reef, Volcano Bay

....

Most coconut-crusted items are covered in shredded coconut (like coconut shrimp), but this chicken is unique in that the coconut is blended and therefore has a more discreet texture that melds perfectly with the rest of the batter. Even those who typically aren't fans of coconut won't help but love the subtle island flavor in this chicken. Complete the meal with fries and coleslaw.

SERVES 6

2 tablespoons salted butter
2 large eggs
1 cup coconut flakes
¼ cup all-purpose flour
½ teaspoon garlic powder
1 teaspoon salt
½ teaspoon ground black
  pepper
6 chicken drumsticks

1. Preheat oven to 425°F. Place butter in a 9" × 13" pan and place in oven while preheating to melt butter.
2. Crack eggs into a small bowl and beat.
3. In a blender, add coconut flakes, flour, garlic powder, salt, and pepper. Pulse until coconut is a fine powder. Pour into a medium dish.
4. Carefully remove hot dish from oven. Working with one drumstick at a time, dip chicken in egg, then roll and pat in coconut mixture, then place in hot dish.
5. Bake 25–30 minutes until thermometer inserted in chicken reads 170°F.
6. Remove to a paper towel–lined plate and serve when cool enough to eat, about 10 minutes. Store leftovers in a sealed container in refrigerator up to 3 days.

 **COOKING TIP**

This dish is typically served with a mango slaw, so if you're inclined, use the recipe for the slaw served on the Jerked Mahi Sandwiches on the following page.

JERKED MAHI SANDWICHES

Kohola Reef, Volcano Bay

....

Mahi-mahi may be available at the fish counter at your local grocer, but if not, check out the freezer section! Frozen fillets of mahi-mahi work great in this dish. Simply let the fish fillets thaw in the refrigerator the day before you plan to use them. Kohola Reef has so many great lunch options; the next time you visit, have each member of your party order something different and share bites. Serve with fries to round out the dish at home.

SERVES 4

FOR JERKED MAHI-MAHI
1 tablespoon dried minced onion
1 teaspoon dried thyme leaves
1 teaspoon ground allspice
1 teaspoon ground black pepper
¼ teaspoon ground cinnamon
¼ teaspoon ground cayenne pepper
½ teaspoon salt
4 (6-ounce) fillets mahi-mahi

FOR CUCUMBER MANGO BASIL SLAW
1 cup thinly sliced napa cabbage
1 cup thinly sliced red cabbage
½ medium ripe mango, peeled, pitted, and cut into thin strips
½ medium cucumber, peeled and cut into thin strips
3 fresh basil leaves, sliced
½ cup shredded carrot

1. To make Jerked Mahi-Mahi: Preheat oven to 450°F. Line a baking sheet with parchment paper and set aside.
2. Mix together minced onion, thyme, allspice, black pepper, cinnamon, cayenne pepper, and salt in a small bowl. Blot fish fillets with a paper towel, then sprinkle seasoning mix all over each fillet. Place on prepared baking sheet.
3. Bake 7–9 minutes or until easily flaked with a fork.
4. To make Cucumber Mango Basil Slaw: In a large bowl, mix together napa cabbage, red cabbage, mango, cucumber, basil, carrot, and cilantro. In a small bowl, combine vinegar, lime juice, vegetable oil, sweet chili sauce, sugar, and sesame oil. Drizzle sauce over slaw and toss to combine. Set aside.

(continued on next page)

¼ cup minced fresh cilantro

1 tablespoon rice vinegar

1 tablespoon lime juice

1 tablespoon vegetable oil

1 tablespoon sweet chili
   sauce

2 teaspoons granulated
   sugar

½ teaspoon sesame oil

FOR ASSEMBLY

4 ciabatta rolls, sliced in half

½ cup salted butter, softened

¼ cup cream of coconut

¼ cup mayonnaise

2 teaspoons sriracha

1 cup shredded iceberg
   lettuce

1 large beefsteak tomato,
   sliced thin

5. To Assemble: Toast ciabatta halves in a toaster. In a small bowl, combine butter and cream of coconut. Spread butter mixture on cut side of each ciabatta half.

6. Mix together mayonnaise and sriracha in a small bowl.

7. Place bottom half of 1 ciabatta roll on a large plate. Add ¼ cup shredded lettuce, 1 or 2 slices tomato, 1 cooked Jerked Mahi-Mahi fillet, ¼ of Cucumber Mango Basil Slaw, and ¼ of sriracha mayonnaise. Add top bun and skewer with a long toothpick. Repeat with remaining ingredients and serve.

COCONUT CURRY CHICKEN

Kohola Reef, Volcano Bay

....

This coconut and plantain dish will take you to a tropical place. Make it any day of the year for a delicious meal the family will love! If you're visiting Volcano Bay, don't miss TeAwa the Fearless River. It is a "lazy" river that is anything but lazy; raging rapids propel your body down the river, with special surprises along the way. Cowabunga!

SERVES 6

FOR COCONUT RICE
2 cups long-grain rice
1 (14-ounce) can unsweetened coconut milk
1 cup water
1 tablespoon granulated sugar
½ teaspoon salt

FOR SWEET PLANTAINS
½ cup vegetable oil
3 large ripe plantains, peeled and cut into 4 pieces each

FOR GREEN CURRY
2 tablespoons coconut oil
3 (4-ounce) boneless, skinless chicken breasts, quartered
1 medium yellow onion, peeled and diced
3 teaspoons minced garlic

1. To make Coconut Rice: Rinse rice in cold water several times. Place in the pot of a rice cooker and add in coconut milk, water, sugar, and salt. Run rice cooker according to manufacturer instructions for white rice. When cooking cycle is done, fluff with a fork and set aside.
2. To make Sweet Plantains: Line a large plate with paper towels. In a medium skillet, heat vegetable oil over medium-high heat 5 minutes. Add plantains and fry 2–3 minutes per side until golden. Remove to paper towel–lined plate and set aside.

1 tablespoon minced fresh
  ginger
2 teaspoons ground
  coriander
1 (14-ounce) can
  unsweetened coconut milk
1 cup shredded carrot
3 tablespoons Thai green
  curry paste
1 teaspoon salt
½ teaspoon ground black
  pepper
2 tablespoons lime juice
1 tablespoon granulated
  sugar
¾ cup chopped fresh cilantro

3. To make Green Curry: In a large skillet over medium heat, add coconut oil and heat 2 minutes, then add chicken quarters and cook 3–4 minutes per side until browned. Remove to a plate.

4. In same pan, add onion and cook 3–4 minutes, stirring frequently, until soft. Stir in garlic, ginger, and coriander and cook 1 minute more.

5. Add in coconut milk, carrot, curry paste, salt, pepper, and browned chicken. Once mixture comes to a boil, reduce heat to low and allow to simmer 5 minutes. Add in lime juice and sugar and stir to combine.

6. Divide Green Curry into six bowls. Add ½ cup Coconut Rice, 2 Sweet Plantain pieces, and 2 tablespoons fresh cilantro to each bowl. Serve immediately.

MANGO BBQ PULLED PORK SANDWICHES

Kohola Reef, Volcano Bay

....

Sometimes less is more....But for this sandwich, more is more! Every element is bursting with tropical flavors and flare, all the way down to the Hawaiian bun. And talk about an easy meal—make the slaw ahead of time and simply allow the pork to cook all day in the slow cooker. Who doesn't like to take some work out of dinner? Serve with fries.

SERVES 6

FOR MANGO PULLED PORK
1 (2-pound) pork shoulder roast
1 tablespoon salt
1 tablespoon ground black pepper
1⅓ teaspoons paprika, divided
¼ cup balsamic vinegar
2¼ cups water, divided
1 large mango, peeled and pitted
1 tablespoon pure honey
1 (18-ounce) bottle original flavor barbecue sauce

1. To make Mango Pulled Pork: Sprinkle pork roast with salt, pepper, and 1 teaspoon paprika and place in a slow cooker. Add balsamic vinegar and 2 cups water to slow cooker and set on low 6 hours.
2. Meanwhile, place mango in a blender with remaining ¼ cup water and blend until smooth. Pour into a small saucepan over medium heat and add honey, remaining ⅓ teaspoon paprika, and barbecue sauce. Bring to a boil, then reduce heat to low and simmer 10 minutes, stirring frequently.
3. After slow cooker cook time is done, strain out liquid from cooker. Add mango barbecue sauce to cooker and cook on high 1 hour.
4. To make Mango Slaw: Combine all ingredients in a medium bowl. Place in refrigerator until ready to use.

(continued on next page)

FOR MANGO SLAW

4 cups tri-colored shredded
    cabbage
3 large mangoes, peeled,
    pitted, and thinly sliced
¼ cup chopped fresh cilantro
2 tablespoons lime juice
2 tablespoons pure honey
½ teaspoon celery salt
½ teaspoon ground black
    pepper

FOR CARAMELIZED PINEAPPLE

2 tablespoons salted butter
6 slices canned pineapple
¼ cup light brown sugar

FOR ASSEMBLY

6 tablespoons salted butter,
    divided
6 Hawaiian burger buns

5. To make Caramelized Pineapple: Melt butter in a large skillet over medium heat. Once melted, add pineapple slices in a single layer in pan. Sprinkle brown sugar on top of slices, cook 3–4 minutes, flip, and cook 3–4 minutes more until dark but not burnt. Remove to a large plate and set aside.

6. To Assemble: Wipe skillet clean and return to stove over medium heat. Melt 1 tablespoon butter in skillet and place two bun halves cut side down into butter to toast. Repeat toasting with remaining butter and buns.

7. Place 1 bottom bun on a large plate. Top with ⅙ of Mango Pulled Pork, 1 slice Caramelized Pineapple, and ⅙ of Mango Slaw. Finish with top bun. Repeat with remaining ingredients and enjoy immediately.

MEATBALL PARMESAN GRILLED CHEESE WITH TOMATO SOUP

Minion Cafe, Universal Studios Hollywood

Minion Cafe has a special quality to it that makes you feel like a kid again. A grilled cheese sandwich with tomato soup is fairly typical comfort food that stirs up childhood memories, but the meatballs and Parmesan elevate this recipe to appease kid and grown-up tastes alike. To make this meal even more impressive, skip the basic canned tomato soup and search the soup aisle for a tomato bisque or something with roasted red peppers or basil included. And take a cue from Minion Cafe by serving this meal with a side of crinkle-cut or curly fries.

SERVES 1

2 tablespoons salted butter, softened

2 slices white bread

½ cup Mexican cheese blend, divided

4 cooked beef meatballs, warmed and halved

2 tablespoons shredded Parmesan cheese

½ cup canned tomato soup, warmed

1. Butter one side of each bread slice. Heat a medium skillet over medium heat 3 minutes, then add 1 bread slice, butter side down. Add ¼ cup Mexican cheese, meatball halves in a single layer, Parmesan cheese, and remaining ¼ cup Mexican cheese. Add second slice of bread, butter side up.

2. Cook 1–2 minutes per side until cheeses are melted and bread is toasted. Serve immediately with tomato soup on the side.

PULLED PORK GRILLED CHEESES WITH BANANA BBQ SAUCE

Minion Cafe, Universal Studios Hollywood

In the Minions and Despicable Me movies, the Minions talk in gibberish. However, one actual word that seems to stick out is "banana." So, Universal decided that Minions are all about bananas, which works perfectly with their yellow bodies! Banana BBQ Sauce is served in this recipe to please Minions and family members alike.

SERVES 3

FOR CARAMELIZED ONION
1 tablespoon olive oil
1 medium white onion, peeled and sliced
1 teaspoon granulated sugar
1 teaspoon salt

FOR BANANA BBQ SAUCE
⅔ cup ketchup
½ cup apple cider vinegar
¼ cup light brown sugar
½ teaspoon paprika
1 teaspoon ground cumin
1 teaspoon salt
1 teaspoon ground black pepper
½ teaspoon banana extract

FOR PULLED PORK GRILLED CHEESES
6 slices white bread
6 tablespoons salted butter, softened
1½ cups shredded sharp Cheddar cheese, divided
¾ cup prepared pulled pork

1. To make Caramelized Onion: Heat a medium skillet over medium heat. Add olive oil and allow to warm 2 minutes. Add onion and sprinkle on sugar and salt and stir to combine. Lower heat to medium-low and allow to brown 30–60 minutes, stirring occasionally. Remove from heat and set aside.

2. To make Banana BBQ Sauce: Combine ketchup, vinegar, brown sugar, paprika, cumin, salt, and pepper in a medium saucepan over medium heat and bring to a boil. Once boiling, reduce heat to low and simmer 5 minutes.

3. Add banana extract and stir well, then pour into three small bowls for serving. Set aside.

4. To make Pulled Pork Grilled Cheeses: Lay out bread slices. Butter sides facing up. In a medium skillet over medium heat, add 1 piece of bread, butter side down. Add ¼ cup cheese, ¼ cup pulled pork, ⅓ of Caramelized Onion, then another ¼ cup cheese. Top with a second slice of bread, butter side up. Allow cheeses to melt and bottom bread to toast, about 2 minutes, then flip and cook 2 minutes more. Both sides of sandwich should be browned, and cheese should be completely melted. Repeat with remaining grilled cheese ingredients.

5. Serve with Banana BBQ Sauce for dipping.

SLOW-ROASTED MOJO JACKFRUIT

Jurassic Cafe, Universal Studios Hollywood

If you're vegan or vegetarian, you've probably already been introduced to the wonder that is jackfruit. This wacky-looking fruit has spikes on the outside and sticky, stringy pulp on the inside. And when cooked using the instructions in this recipe, something magical happens: It tastes and feels just like pulled pork! Mojo is a traditional sauce that is common throughout Central America and the Caribbean, perfect for the Jurassic World theme of Universal Studios Hollywood. Complete the meal with sides of black beans and rice.

SERVES 6

¾ cup pulp-free orange juice
¼ cup lime juice
4 teaspoons minced garlic
1 teaspoon ground cumin
1 teaspoon dried oregano
1 tablespoon dried cilantro
1 (20-ounce) can jackfruit in brine, drained and cored
6 (4") corn tortillas
6 tablespoons dairy-free sour cream
6 tablespoons dairy-free pepper jack "cheese"

1. Blend orange juice, lime juice, garlic, cumin, oregano, and cilantro in a blender until combined and smooth. Pour into a large container, add jackfruit, cover, and allow to marinate in refrigerator 30 minutes up to overnight.
2. Pour contents of container into a pressure cooker and set to pressure cook 8 minutes. Allow pressure to naturally release 10 minutes, then manually release remaining pressure.
3. Remove jackfruit from pot with tongs and place in a large bowl. Shred with forks.
4. Set pressure cooker to the "sauté" setting to allow sauce to reduce and thicken 5 minutes. Return jackfruit to pot and stir into sauce.
5. To serve, scoop jackfruit onto tortillas. Squeeze on dairy-free sour cream and sprinkle with dairy-free cheese.

KRUSTY BURGER

Krusty Burger, Universal Studios Hollywood

Krusty Burger is the fictional burger joint owned by Krusty the Clown in *The Simpsons*. Krusty ran a promotion that gave free Krusty Burgers to anyone who could pick the Olympic events won by the United States of America. Because of a boycott, the Soviet Union pulled out of the Olympics and the United States won most events. Because Universal is unlikely to make the same blunder, learn how to make Krusty Burgers at home so you can have them anytime!

SERVES 1

FOR SECRET SAUCE
½ cup mayonnaise
2 tablespoons peeled and minced yellow onion
1 tablespoon ketchup
1 tablespoon sweet pickle relish
½ teaspoon lemon juice
½ teaspoon paprika
¼ teaspoon salt

FOR BURGER
1 (⅓-pound) beef patty
½ teaspoon salt
¼ teaspoon ground black pepper

FOR ASSEMBLY
1 white hamburger bun
2 tablespoons nacho cheese sauce
2 medium leaves iceberg lettuce
1 large slice beefsteak tomato
1 small sweet pickle
1 cup cooked seasoned curly fries

1. To make Secret Sauce: Combine all ingredients in a small bowl. Leftovers can be stored in an airtight container in refrigerator up to 1 week.

2. To make Burger: Season patty with salt and pepper. Heat a small skillet over medium heat 2 minutes, then add patty. Cook 3–4 minutes until underside is browned and cooked, then flip and cook an additional 3-4 minutes until internal temperature reaches 160°F. Remove from heat and set aside.

3. To Assemble: Place bottom bun on a large plate. Add cooked patty, followed by nacho cheese sauce, lettuce, then tomato. Drizzle with Secret Sauce and finish with top bun. Drive a toothpick through top of burger bun and add sweet pickle to top of toothpick. Serve immediately with curly fries on the side.

UNIVERSAL PARKS TIP

Next time you're at Universal Studios Florida or Universal Studios Hollywood, take some time to check out the details around Springfield. You never know what characters you'll see or what might happen when you press an enticing button!

TROPICAL ROASTED CHICKEN SALAD

Jurassic Cafe, Universal Studios Hollywood

Whether at the theme park or at home, if you're looking for something light and fresh, look no further. This salad delivers a pop of citrus and great lean protein to keep you moving. If you want to make this salad to pack in a work lunch, simply make the dressing ahead of time and put it in a small sealed container, then mix the greens together with the chicken and put the pomegranate, avocado, and queso fresco in bags. When you're ready to eat, mix them all together.

SERVES 1

FOR CITRUS VINAIGRETTE
¾ cup olive oil
⅓ cup apple cider vinegar
3 tablespoons lemon juice
3 tablespoons pulp-free orange juice
4 tablespoons granulated sugar
Zest of ½ medium lemon
1 teaspoon salt
½ teaspoon ground black pepper

FOR SALAD
1 cup shredded iceberg lettuce
1 cup shredded angel hair coleslaw
½ cup shredded cooked skinless rotisserie chicken
2 tablespoons pomegranate arils
2 tablespoons grated queso fresco
½ medium avocado, peeled, pitted, and sliced

1. To make Citrus Vinaigrette: Add all ingredients to a small bowl or Mason jar. Mix or shake well. Dressing will last in sealed container up to 1 week in refrigerator.
2. To make Salad: Lay down shredded lettuce and cabbage on a large plate. Top with chicken and drizzle with Citrus Vinaigrette. Sprinkle on pomegranate arils and queso fresco. Lay sliced avocado to side of salad. Serve.

CHAPTER 6

SUGAR CONFECTIONS

Universal Parks have a plethora of sweet treats, so this book divides them into two categories: sugar confections and desserts. Sugar confections include the more candy-like items, while desserts consist of ice creams and cakes. Of course, when it comes to sugary goodies, the line can be very thin, so feel free to peruse both this chapter as well as Chapter 7 when looking for a little something-something to appease a sweet tooth.

In this chapter, you'll discover confections inspired by your favorite characters, like Minion Apples, as well as recipes you've seen in film series, like Felix Felicis from Harry Potter. And don't overlook the new favorites waiting to be discovered, like the Spiced Cashew Brittle sold at Universal Studios Hollywood. Wherever your hankerings for sweets guide you, enjoy the ride (and the sugar!).

MINION APPLES

San Francisco Candy Factory, Universal Studios Florida

The juicy Minion Apple satisfies any sweet tooth—Minion or otherwise—while still giving you a serving of fruit! And the portable aspect makes it perfect for a Minion dance party. You can hold your own Minion dance party at home anytime: Just cue up the soundtrack to any of the Despicable Me or Minions movies on your speakers and bust a move.

YIELDS 3 APPLES

11 ounces baking caramels
1 tablespoon water
3 large Granny Smith apples
1½ cups white chocolate chips
1 teaspoon coconut oil
5 drops yellow gel food coloring
1 (0.75-ounce) tube black gel icing
1 (0.75-ounce) tube gray gel icing

1. Line a baking sheet with parchment paper and grease paper with nonstick cooking spray. Set aside.
2. Pour caramels into a medium microwave-safe bowl and add water. Microwave 2–3 minutes, stirring after each minute, until caramels are melted entirely.
3. Make sure outside of apples is dry. Drive an ice pop stick or wooden dowel into top (stem part) of each apple. Dip and roll each apple in caramel, scraping excess from bottom, and place on prepared baking sheet with stick poking straight up. Allow to set in refrigerator 30 minutes.
4. Pour white chocolate chips and coconut oil into a medium microwave-safe bowl and microwave 2–4 minutes, stirring every 30 seconds, until chocolate just melts. Scoop a little melted chocolate into three 1" circular chocolate molds and allow to set in refrigerator 1 hour. Stir yellow food coloring into remaining white chocolate.

(continued on next page)

5. Dip and roll each caramel-coated apple in yellow chocolate, scraping excess from bottom, and replace on prepared baking sheet. Allow to set at room temperature 1 hour.

6. Squeeze a dollop of black gel icing on center front of each apple to use as adhesive for white chocolate circles, then attach white circles to apple for Minion eyes. Squirt a pea-sized black icing dot on center of each white circle and outline outer white circle in gray icing. Add a black "strap" for the eye goggle, little black lines of hair on top of apple, and a black smile under eye. Allow icing to set, about 30 minutes, then enjoy.

UNIVERSAL PARKS TIP

If you love the Minions and want to ride along on their attraction but don't love wild jerking, ask a Universal employee if you may sit in a nonmoving seat. These seats are available in the back corner of the room.

BUTTER PECAN FUDGE

San Francisco Candy Factory, Universal Studios Florida

....

San Francisco Candy Factory is located across from the exit to the Fast & Furious–Supercharged attraction. A large confection counter holds all kinds of fresh goodies, from fudge to cookies to caramel apples. This fudge is creamy and classic and will become a go-to recipe in your home.

YIELDS 16 PIECES

1 cup salted butter
1 cup granulated sugar
1 cup light brown sugar
1 cup heavy whipping cream
½ teaspoon salt
2 teaspoons vanilla extract
4 cups confectioners' sugar
2 cups pecan halves

1. Grease an 8" × 8" baking dish with nonstick cooking spray and set aside.
2. In a large saucepan over medium heat, add butter, granulated sugar, brown sugar, cream, and salt. Stir to combine and bring to a boil. Once boiling, allow to boil 4 minutes while stirring frequently.
3. Remove pan from heat and add vanilla and confectioners' sugar. Stir until smooth. Fold in pecan halves and pour mixture into prepared pan, smoothing top. Refrigerate to set, 3-5 hours. Cut into squares to serve. Leftovers can be covered with plastic wrap and refrigerated up to 1 week.

 **MIX IT UP**

Not everyone loves pecans, so if they aren't your favorite, sub in what you love! Walnuts, peanuts, and macadamia nuts would work great. And if you are allergic or don't like nuts at all, just omit them entirely!

BLUE CAMO FUDGE

San Francisco Candy Factory, Universal Studios Florida

Blue Camo Fudge might seem like a nod to the Universal property Transformers based on where it is currently sold, but was actually part of the culinary offerings to promote the opening of Velocicoaster from Jurassic World. "Blue" is the name of one of the vicious velociraptors who inhabit the paddock that houses the Velocicoaster. Enjoy this yummy and eye-catching fudge beyond reach of dinosaurs.

YIELDS 16 PIECES

4 cups white chocolate chips, divided
1⅓ cups sweetened condensed milk, divided
1 teaspoon lemon extract
½ teaspoon salt, divided
1 teaspoon raspberry extract
5 drops blue gel food coloring, divided

1. Line an 8" × 8" baking dish with parchment paper and set aside.
2. Pour 2 cups white chocolate chips and ⅔ cup sweetened condensed milk into a large microwave-safe bowl and microwave 1 minute, 30 seconds at 70 percent power. Stir well. Add lemon extract and ¼ teaspoon salt and stir to combine. Set aside.
3. In a separate large microwave-safe bowl, add remaining 2 cups white chocolate chips and remaining ⅔ cup sweetened condensed milk and microwave 1 minute, 30 seconds at 70 percent power. Stir well. Add raspberry extract and remaining ¼ teaspoon salt and stir to combine. Pour half of raspberry mixture into a medium bowl. Mix 2 drops food coloring into one bowl to get a light blue mixture, and mix remaining 3 drops food coloring into the other bowl to get a dark blue mixture.
4. Using separate spoons for each mixture, plop alternating scoops of white, light blue, and dark blue mixtures into prepared pan to create a "camo" pattern. Once all mixture has been used up, place pan in refrigerator to set 4–6 hours until hard. Cut into sixteen squares and serve.

MILK CHOCOLATE PECAN PATTIES

San Francisco Candy Factory, Universal Studios Florida

Known perhaps more commonly as a "turtle," this indulgent little treat has got it all: It's salty, sweet, chewy, and chocolaty. What else could you want? If you want to get wild with it, try mixing up some of these ingredients. Add in walnuts, peanuts, or macadamia nuts. Sub white chocolate chips for the milk chocolate chips. Top them with sprinkles. The choice is all yours!

YIELDS 6–8 PATTIES

1½ cups whole pecans
¼ cup salted butter
½ cup light brown sugar
¼ cup light corn syrup
4 ounces sweetened
   condensed milk
½ teaspoon vanilla extract
¾ cup milk chocolate chips
1 teaspoon coconut oil

1. Line a baking sheet with parchment paper and draw 3" circles evenly across paper with a pencil. Flip paper over on sheet. Spray paper with nonstick cooking spray. Lay pecans in a single layer within each circle. Set aside.
2. In a medium saucepan over medium heat, add butter, brown sugar, and corn syrup. Bring to a boil, then add sweetened condensed milk and vanilla. Maintain heat, stirring frequently, until mixture reaches 245°F on a candy thermometer.
3. Carefully spoon caramel into center of each circle on top of pecans. Allow to set at room temperature, about 45 minutes.
4. Pour chocolate chips and coconut oil into a small microwave-safe bowl and microwave in 30-second increments, stirring between cook times, until chips just melt. Spoon chocolate onto center of caramels and smooth into circles.
5. Allow to set at room temperature 1 hour before serving. Leftovers can be stored in an airtight container at room temperature up to 5 days.

LOVE POTION

Weasleys' Wizard Wheezes, Universal Studios Florida

Love Potion, or "Amortentia," is a powerful agent of magic in the Harry Potter books and movies, as it causes the drinker to be intensely infatuated and obsessive. The scent of the potion morphs and changes to match whatever the subject loves best. What would your scent be? This recipe uses the lovely aromas of succulent roses and honey. Enjoy in small quantities because the flavor is powerful!

SERVES 4

4 tablespoons corn syrup
1 tablespoon rose water
1 tablespoon pure honey

Combine all ingredients in a small bowl. Decant into four small vials or bottles and serve.

 **COOKING TIP**

If you can't find rose water at your local grocery store, try an online retailer. The rose smell and taste are iconic to this Universal recipe and shouldn't be skipped!

FAINTING FANCIES

Weasleys' Wizard Wheezes, Universal Studios Florida

Sold by the Weasley twins in the Harry Potter books and movies, the original version of this confection makes the eater faint right on the spot. Luckily, the sweet candies you make with this recipe will *not* cause fainting!

YIELDS 1 DOZEN FANCIES

1 ounce pulp-free orange juice
3 teaspoons gelatin powder, divided
1 ounce lemon juice
¾ cup granulated sugar, divided
¼ cup water
2 tablespoons light corn syrup

1. Grease a mold with twelve or more shallow 2" circle divots with nonstick cooking spray and set aside.
2. Add orange juice and 1½ teaspoons gelatin powder to a small bowl. Add lemon juice and remaining 1½ teaspoons gelatin powder to another small bowl. Stir each well and set aside.
3. In a small saucepan over medium heat, add ½ cup sugar, water, and corn syrup. Bring to a boil, then allow to boil until temperature on a candy thermometer reads 234°F.
4. Pour half of hot mixture into orange juice mixture and other half into lemon juice mixture. Stir well to combine.
5. Strain each mixture through a mesh sieve separately. Fill six divots of prepared mold with orange juice mixture and six divots with lemon juice mixture. Carefully place in refrigerator to set, about 4 hours up to overnight.

(continued on next page)

6. When confections are set, remove from mold to a large plate greased with nonstick cooking spray. Using kitchen shears, snip each circle in half. Press an orange half to a lemon half at their center seams. Repeat with remaining halves. Dip each Fancy in remaining ¼ cup sugar to coat. Serve.

 **COOKING TIP**

This recipe and the following three are part of a collection called Skiving Snackboxes and are sold individually or as a full set at Universal. The Skiving Snackbox was referenced in the Harry Potter books and movies as a collection of trick candies imbued with spells to make the eater sick and able to "skive off," or leave class or work. You can make just one, or all four recipes together!

NOSEBLEED NOUGAT

Weasleys' Wizard Wheezes, Universal Studios Florida

The Weasley family is well known in the Harry Potter books and movies for its "pure blood," red hair, and lack of money. Twins Fred and George decided they wanted to break from this last label and turn their silly and mischievous nature into a lucrative business. Thus, Weasleys' Wizard Wheezes was born, providing witches and wizards with the hijinks of their dreams. This Nosebleed Nougat recipe is delicious and stunning, and skips the magical spell needed for a nosebleed.

YIELDS 18 PIECES

FOR NOUGAT
2 cups granulated sugar
1½ cups pure honey
2 tablespoons water
2 teaspoons vanilla extract
4 large egg whites
¾ cup confectioners' sugar

FOR CHOCOLATE COATING
3 cups milk chocolate chips
3 teaspoons coconut oil

FOR ASSEMBLY
72 white chocolate crunchy pearls
54 shelled pistachios

1. To make Nougat: In a medium saucepan over medium heat, add granulated sugar, honey, water, and vanilla. Stir frequently until temperature reaches 300°F on a candy thermometer.
2. While sugar mixture is cooking, in the bowl of a stand mixer fitted with a whisk attachment, beat egg whites at high speed until stiff peaks form, about 4 minutes.
3. Once sugar mixture is at 300°F, ladle a slow, steady stream into egg whites while continuing to beat at high speed. Keep beating an additional 5 minutes until mixture is glossy and white. Add confectioners' sugar and whisk until fully incorporated.
4. Grease a 9" × 13" pan with nonstick cooking spray, lay down parchment paper in pan, and grease parchment paper with nonstick cooking spray. Grease a spatula with nonstick cooking spray.

(continued on next page)

5. Use a spatula to scoop nougat into prepared pan and smooth out in an even layer. Allow to set at room temperature 8 hours up to overnight.

6. Once nougat is set, remove from pan and slice into 3" × 2" rectangles with a knife greased with nonstick cooking spray.

7. To make Chocolate Coating: Place chocolate chips and coconut oil in a small microwave-safe bowl and microwave 30 seconds, stir, then microwave 30 seconds more and stir, repeating until chocolate chips are melted and smooth.

8. Grease a baking sheet with nonstick cooking spray. Blot nougat pieces with a paper towel to remove excess grease, dip each in melted chocolate, and place on prepared baking sheet.

9. While chocolate is still wet, place 4 white chocolate crunchy pearls at one end of each nougat piece, in a 2 × 2 pattern, and place 3 pistachios in a line on the other end. Refrigerate 1 hour, then serve.

FEVER FUDGE

Weasleys' Wizard Wheezes, Universal Studios Florida

If you want to change up the cinnamon flavor in this delectable fudge, just swap out the cinnamon jelly beans for whatever flavor you prefer! If you want to go even more wild, swap out the vanilla extract in the fudge and try something new, like almond extract, maple extract, or even banana extract. The combinations are endless!

YIELDS 16 PIECES

4 cups white chocolate chips
1⅓ cups sweetened
   condensed milk
2 teaspoons vanilla extract
½ teaspoon salt
5 drops blue gel food
   coloring
½ cup cinnamon jelly beans

1. Line an 8" × 8" baking dish with parchment paper and set aside.
2. Pour white chocolate chips and sweetened condensed milk into a large microwave-safe bowl and microwave 1 minute, 30 seconds at 70 percent power. Stir well. Add vanilla and salt and stir to combine. Stir in food coloring. Stir in jelly beans.
3. Pour batter into prepared baking dish. Allow to set in refrigerator 4–6 hours or until hard. Cut into sixteen squares and serve.

PUKING PASTILLES

Weasleys' Wizard Wheezes, Universal Studios Florida

In the Harry Potter series, this candy, the last item found in the Skiving Snackbox at Weasleys' Wizard Wheezes, makes the user vomit so they can get out of class. Luckily, the antidote is located right on the same pastille (another name for "candy"). By eating the opposite end, you can make the vomiting stop. In the Harry Potter novels, the candies were orange and purple, but as seen in the movies, and subsequently in the Universal Theme Parks, the coloring was changed to green and purple (green as the puking end and purple as the antidote). Don't worry: The following recipe won't make you queasy! It's all the delicious sugary goodness of the Harry Potter sweet with none of the nausea.

YIELDS 36 PASTILLES

3¾ cups granulated sugar
1½ cups light corn syrup
1 cup water
½ teaspoon baking powder
5 drops purple gel food coloring
5 drops green gel food coloring

1. In a medium saucepan over medium heat, combine sugar, corn syrup, and water. Stir until sugar dissolves, 2–3 minutes. Use a spatula to scrape down any sugar granules along the walls of the saucepan.
2. Allow mixture to come to 300°F on a candy thermometer. Do not stir during this step.
3. Remove pot from heat and stir in baking powder. Quickly and carefully pour half of mixture into a second small pot. Stir purple food coloring into one pot and green into the other pot.
4. Moving quickly, simultaneously spoon purple and green mixtures into opposite sides of one diamond divot in a 36-divot silicone mold. Continue with remaining mixtures and divots. Allow to set at room temperature 1 hour before removing from mold and enjoying.

CHOCOLATE AND BANANA COTTON CANDY

Super Silly Stuff, Universal Studios Hollywood

Not every grocery store carries every flavor of floss sugar, but many online retailers have these flavors at low prices and with quick shipping. If you don't have a cotton candy machine, these can also be found in inexpensive varieties online. Most treats in Super Silly Fun Land at Universal are banana flavored, in homage to the Minions, who don't quite speak English, but seem to always know the word "banana."

SERVES 1

1 tablespoon banana floss sugar
1 tablespoon chocolate floss sugar

1. Preheat cotton candy machine.
2. Following manufacturer instructions, add banana floss sugar and collect cotton candy with a paper cone, moving your hand in a swirling motion. Scrunch cotton candy off the cone and place into a small bowl or bucket.
3. Repeat with chocolate floss sugar, scrunching chocolate cotton candy on top of banana cotton candy. Enjoy immediately.

SPICED CASHEW BRITTLE

City Snack Shop, Universal Studios Hollywood

....

City Snack Shop is a little window a bit off the main thoroughfare of Universal Studios Hollywood. This crispy brittle can be enjoyed as you wait in line nearby for the Secret Life of Pets: Off the Leash attraction, or made in bulk as a gift for friends. Simply make a double batch in a 9" × 13" pan and put a few pieces each in several cellophane bags. It is sure to brighten someone's day!

SERVES 2

¾ cup granulated sugar
¼ cup light corn syrup
½ cup water
½ teaspoon salt
1 teaspoon baking soda
½ teaspoon ground cinnamon
⅛ teaspoon ground nutmeg
¾ cup unsalted whole cashews

1. Grease an 8" × 8" baking dish lightly with nonstick cooking spray. Set aside.
2. In a medium saucepan over medium heat, add sugar, corn syrup, water, and salt. Cook while stirring 4 minutes, making sure to scrape sides with a spatula to remove sugar crystals. Then allow mixture to rise to 300°F on a candy thermometer (do not stir).
3. Meanwhile, combine baking soda, cinnamon, and nutmeg in a small bowl. When sugar mixture reaches 300°F, remove from heat and stir in spice blend. Mixture will puff up. Quickly fold in cashews.
4. Pour into prepared baking dish and use a greased spatula to smooth out top. Allow to cool at least 1 hour or until brittle is hard to the touch.
5. Release brittle from dish and smash into pieces. Brittle can be stored in an airtight container at room temperature up to 1 week.

NO MELT ICE CREAM

Honeydukes, Islands of Adventure

Honeydukes is not only an adventure for the taste buds, but for the eyes as well. Pinks and greens adorn every nook and cranny, and bright packaging decorates every treat. No Melt Ice Cream makes the perfect Harry Potter party treat, as you can set it out for an hour and not fear it melting!

SERVES 2

½ cup salted butter, softened
1 cup confectioners' sugar
½ teaspoon vanilla extract
1 teaspoon cornstarch
1 teaspoon heavy whipping
   cream
2 teaspoons rainbow
   sprinkles
2 maraschino cherries

1. In the bowl of a stand mixer fitted with a paddle attachment, cream butter and confectioners' sugar. Add vanilla and cornstarch. Mix. Slowly add in cream while mixing, adding more if needed to achieve a creamy consistency.
2. Scoop "ice cream" into a piping bag fitted with a large star tip and squeeze into two small martini glasses. Sprinkle with rainbow sprinkles and top each glass with a maraschino cherry. Serve.

 **MIX IT UP**

Universal sells No Melt Ice Cream in several flavors. If you want to create one of the other flavors, just swap out the vanilla extract for the flavor of your choice. To take it a step further, you can add some gel food coloring to match the flavor and decorate with special toppings!

FELIX FELICIS

Honeydukes, Islands of Adventure

Felix Felicis is a much-sought-after potion in the Harry Potter books and movies, as it gives the drinker incredible luck for one whole day. Universal Parks imagined this to taste like honey and ginger and package it up in a teardrop-shaped vial just as it is portrayed in the Harry Potter films. Just like with the Love Potion (see recipe in this chapter), drink this in small sips as it can be strong!

SERVES 4

2 tablespoons grated fresh ginger
½ cup amber honey

1. In a small saucepan over medium heat, add ginger and honey. Bring to a boil, then reduce heat to low and simmer 15 minutes.
2. Strain mixture through a sieve into a small bowl and allow to cool at room temperature, about 2 hours. Decant into vials.

CHAPTER 7

DESSERTS

While Chapter 6 focused on sugar confections, this chapter is all about classic desserts like ice creams, cakes, and cookies. The movies provide endless treats—and inspiration for inventive recipes—to enjoy, and Universal has not missed out on this opportunity.

In the following chapter, you'll find easy-to-follow recipes for mouthwatering goodies such as the super-portable Sundaes on a Stick, the *Instagram*mable Nutella Banana Pudding, and the classic Pineapple Dole Whip served at Schwab's Pharmacy. Whether you are making these dishes for a crowd or whipping up a little sweet for one, you'll find just what you need to settle a craving. Re-create a favorite, or check out something you've never tried or even heard of before. Universal Parks are all about daring, so *get daring* and embark on an exciting dessert journey in your kitchen!

STRAWBERRY AND PEANUT BUTTER ICE CREAM

Florean Fortescue's Ice Cream Parlor, Universal Studios Florida

The book *Harry Potter and the Prisoner of Azkaban* describes Harry Potter's summer stay at the lodgings above the Leaky Cauldron. During those three weeks, he spends afternoons hanging out at Florean Fortescue's Ice Cream Parlor, with Mr. Fortescue himself serving Harry free ice cream sundaes every half hour and helping him complete his homework. Holding all the nostalgic flavors of the popular childhood sandwich, this treat enjoyed by Harry is both refreshing and rich at the same time.

SERVES 6

2 cups hulled and sliced strawberries
1 cup granulated sugar, divided
2 cups heavy whipping cream
1 cup whole milk
½ teaspoon vanilla extract
½ teaspoon salt
½ cup creamy peanut butter

1. Combine strawberries and ½ cup sugar in a medium bowl and allow to sit 15 minutes for juices to release.
2. Pour contents of bowl into a blender and blend until smooth. Strain through a medium-mesh sieve into a large bowl.
3. Add remaining ½ cup sugar, cream, milk, vanilla, and salt to bowl and whisk to combine.
4. Scoop peanut butter into a small microwave-safe bowl and microwave 30–60 seconds until soft and runny. Pour into cream mixture and whisk to combine.
5. Pour mixture into an ice cream machine and run according to manufacturer's instructions 15–20 minutes or until thick and creamy.
6. Scoop ice cream into a large freezer-safe container, cover, and freeze 4 hours up to overnight. Serve.

MILE HIGH APPLE PIE

Richter's Burger Co., Universal Studios Florida

....

This apple pie is simple and delicious. If you have extra apples of any kind that are going to go soft soon, whip up this recipe instead of sending them to the garbage. Serve a slice with a scoop of vanilla ice cream or piled a mile high with canned whipped cream.

YIELDS 1 (9") PIE

½ cup light brown sugar
½ cup granulated sugar
1 tablespoon all-purpose flour
1 teaspoon ground cinnamon
8 cups peeled, cored, and sliced Granny Smith apples
1 (2-count) box refrigerated pie crusts
1 large egg, beaten

1. Preheat oven to 425°F. Grease a 9" pie pan with nonstick cooking spray and set aside.
2. In a large bowl, combine brown sugar, granulated sugar, flour, and cinnamon. Add apple slices and toss to coat well.
3. Unroll 1 pie crust and place in prepared pie pan. Pour in coated apples and top with second crust, crimping edges together. Poke four small holes in top crust to vent and brush top with beaten egg.
4. Bake 35–45 minutes until top is golden brown and filling is bubbling. Allow to cool to room temperature, about 1 hour. Slice and serve.

PINEAPPLE DOLE WHIP

Schwab's Pharmacy, Universal Studios Florida

....

Pineapple Dole Whip is well known as a Disney Parks staple and has literal fandoms based around it. Universal Parks wanted in on the action and serves authentic Pineapple Dole Whip at Schwab's Pharmacy. The Pharmacy is a re-creation of the original Schwab's Pharmacy located on Sunset Boulevard in the 1930s, where actors and producers would hang out for a sweet treat. Pineapple Dole Whip is fruity and refreshing and easy and fun to make at home. Try "whipping" up a batch for the family to enjoy together!

SERVES 4

1 cup water
1½ cups granulated sugar
2 cups chilled pineapple juice
1 tablespoon lime juice

1. In a medium microwave-safe bowl, combine water and sugar. Microwave 1 minute, stir, then microwave an additional 1 minute and stir. Cover and refrigerate 2 hours up to overnight.
2. In a separate medium bowl, add pineapple juice, lime juice, and ½ cup chilled syrup. Stir to combine. Pour into an ice cream machine and run according to manufacturer's instructions 20 minutes or until creamy.
3. Portion into four bowls and serve immediately, or transfer to a large freezer-safe plastic container, cover, and freeze overnight for a harder consistency.

SUNDAES ON A STICK

Hop on Pop Ice Cream Shop, Islands of Adventure

Employees at Hop on Pop Ice Cream Shop actually make these treats fresh and prepared to order right in front of your eyes! They have ice cream already frozen on the wooden stick, but then they dip it in the chocolate and cover it in your desired toppings. You can simulate this experience at home by creating a made-to-order Sundaes on a Stick station! Bring out the frozen ice creams on a stick one at a time from the freezer and take orders from your family and friends as to what toppings they would like on their bars. Fun and yummy!

SERVES 4

¼ **gallon vanilla ice cream**
¾ **cup milk chocolate chips**
4 **tablespoons salted butter**
¼ **cup vegetable oil**
¼ **cup toppings of choice (rainbow sprinkles, cookie crumbles, nuts, etc.)**

1. Allow vanilla ice cream to soften at room temperature 10–20 minutes or until soft enough to work with. Scoop softened ice cream into ice pop molds and insert wooden sticks. Allow to harden completely in freezer, 6 hours up to overnight.
2. In a medium microwave-safe bowl, add chocolate chips and butter. Microwave 30 seconds, stir, then microwave 30 seconds more. Continue cooking and stirring until chocolate chips just melt. Add oil and whisk well to combine. Allow to cool to room temperature, stirring occasionally, about 10 minutes.
3. Unmold hardened ice cream and drizzle with chocolate sauce. Sprinkle with topping of choice and enjoy immediately.

SIMPLIFICATION HACK

If you don't want to wait for ice cream to freeze, just buy a box of plain chocolate-coated ice cream bars and add the toppings! Drizzle a light amount of melted chocolate onto the bars first to help the toppings adhere better.

PUMPKIN CAKES

Honeydukes, Islands of Adventure

Oddly enough, even though these are called Pumpkin Cakes, they have no pumpkin or pumpkin flavor in them. They simply look like pumpkins! An adorable little treat that would work just as well for a Harry Potter party or a Halloween occasion, these eye-catching blends of vanilla and spice flavors will have you wanting to eat the whole pumpkin patch.

YIELDS 20 CAKES

FOR CAKES
1 cup light brown sugar
⅓ cup vegetable oil
⅓ cup salted butter, softened
2 large eggs
1 teaspoon vanilla extract
½ cup whole milk
1½ cups all-purpose flour
½ teaspoon baking powder
½ teaspoon baking soda
½ teaspoon salt
1½ teaspoons ground cinnamon
½ teaspoon ground nutmeg
½ teaspoon ground ginger
¼ teaspoon ground allspice
¼ teaspoon ground cloves

1. To make Cakes: Preheat oven to 350°F. Spray two twenty-cup Bundtlette pans with nonstick cooking spray and set aside.
2. In the bowl of a stand mixer fitted with a paddle attachment, cream together brown sugar, oil, butter, eggs, vanilla, and milk about 2 minutes or until well combined. Add in flour, baking powder, baking soda, salt, cinnamon, nutmeg, ginger, allspice, and cloves and stir 1 minute to combine.
3. Scoop batter into a piping bag or plastic bag with one corner snipped off. Pipe batter into prepared pans, filling each divot almost to the top.
4. Bake 8–10 minutes until a toothpick inserted in cakes comes out clean. Allow to rest in pans 10 minutes, then turn out onto a wire rack and allow to cool completely, about 45 minutes.

(continued on next page)

FOR FROSTING
2 cups confectioners' sugar
3 tablespoons water
2 tablespoons meringue powder
2 drops yellow gel food coloring
2 drops red gel food coloring

FOR ASSEMBLY
4 strands black licorice

5. To make Frosting: Combine all ingredients in a medium bowl. Color should be pumpkin orange; adjust food coloring amounts accordingly.
6. To Assemble: Place 1 Cake inverted onto wire rack. Wipe a small amount of Frosting onto flat surface of cake and place a second Cake flat side down onto Frosting. Scoop or pour Frosting over cake to cover bottom and top. Snip licorice into 1" segments and place 1 piece in top of frosted cake. Repeat with remaining ingredients.
7. Allow Frosting to dry completely, about 45 minutes. Serve.

LAVENDER BLUEBERRY PANNA COTTA

Mythos Restaurant, Islands of Adventure

....

"Panna cotta" is an Italian term that translates to "cooked cream." Very much like a flan or crème brûlée, panna cotta is a cream mixture made in a mold. It holds its shape on its own. While Mythos is primarily focused on Greek gods, the restaurant has several nods to Roman gods as well, like this Italian dessert.

SERVES 6

FOR PANNA COTTA
1 (7-gram) envelope gelatin powder
¼ cup water
1¼ cups heavy whipping cream
¾ cup granulated sugar, divided
1 teaspoon dried lavender flowers
¾ cup fresh blueberries
1 cup whole milk

1. To make Panna Cotta: Grease a jumbo muffin tin with nonstick cooking spray and set aside.
2. Sprinkle gelatin in a small bowl, add ¼ cup water, and stir. Allow to sit and soak 10 minutes.
3. Meanwhile, in a small saucepan over medium heat, combine cream, sugar, lavender flowers, and blueberries. Cook while stirring frequently 4–5 minutes until combined and hot. Use a potato masher to squish blueberries.
4. Pour mixture through a fine-mesh sieve into a large bowl, add gelatin mixture, and stir.
5. Warm milk in a small microwave-safe bowl in microwave 30 seconds, stir, then microwave 30 seconds more. Pour milk into blueberry mixture and stir to combine. Divide mixture into six jumbo muffin divots and place in refrigerator to set, about 4 hours.

(continued on next page)

FOR RASPBERRY SYRUP
3 cups fresh raspberries
1 cup water
½ cup granulated sugar
1 teaspoon vanilla extract

FOR ASSEMBLY
3 fresh blueberries
3 fresh raspberries
3 edible yellow flowers
1 tablespoon granola

6. To make Raspberry Syrup: Combine raspberries, water, and sugar in a small saucepan over medium heat. Bring to a boil, then cook 15 minutes. Mash with a potato masher.

7. Strain through a fine-mesh sieve into a small bowl and add vanilla, then stir. Allow to cool at room temperature, about 2 hours.

8. To Assemble: Turn out Panna Cottas from muffin tin and place each in its own shallow dish. Spoon Raspberry Syrup around base and add blueberries, raspberries, and edible flowers around base. Sprinkle granola over top of Panna Cotta and serve immediately.

DULCE DE LECHE CHURROS

Natural Selections, Islands of Adventure

If you can't find pre-toasted coconut at the store, it is easy to toast coconut at home in the microwave! Spread the coconut in a thin layer in an 8" × 8" microwave-safe glass dish. Microwave on high 4–5 minutes, stirring after each minute, until the coconut is toasty and browned. Remove from microwave and allow to cool, about 15 minutes. Voilà! Dulce de leche is a caramelly sauce common in Central and South America—a tasty homage to Jurassic Park, which is set off of Costa Rica.

YIELDS 6 CHURROS

1 cup water

3 tablespoons granulated sugar

½ teaspoon salt

3 tablespoons plus 6 cups vegetable oil, divided

1 cup all-purpose flour

6 tablespoons dulce de leche sauce

6 tablespoons toasted coconut

1. Line a baking sheet with parchment paper and set aside.
2. In a medium saucepan over medium-high heat, add water, sugar, salt, and 3 tablespoons oil. Stir until mixture reaches a boil (about 4 minutes), then remove from heat.
3. Add flour and stir until combined. Scoop into a large piping bag fitted with a large star tip. Let dough cool until able to handle, about 10 minutes.
4. Pipe dough into six 6" lines on prepared baking sheet. Place in freezer to set 1 hour.
5. In a large pot over medium heat, heat remaining 48 ounces oil to 375°F. Line a large plate with paper towels and set aside.
6. Carefully slide 1 or 2 churros into oil and fry, while turning, 1–2 minutes until golden brown and cooked through. Remove to paper towel–lined plate and repeat with remaining churros.
7. Allow churros to cool completely, about 30 minutes, then drizzle each with 1 tablespoon dulce de leche sauce and sprinkle with 1 tablespoon toasted coconut. Enjoy immediately.

FUNNEL PUFFS

Comic Strip Cafe, Islands of Adventure

....

Toon Lagoon is loaded with water activities of all sorts, including Dudley Do-Right's Ripsaw Falls log ride, Popeye & Bluto's Bilge-Rat Barges raft ride, and Me Ship, The Olive play area. If you're wetter than you had hoped, just pay a few bucks to step into a heating chamber and dry off those clothes. But I would rather spend my bucks on a hot plate of Funnel Puffs and warm up from the inside out! Perfect at home any day of the year, it's an easy treat to whip up.

SERVES 2

48 ounces plus 1 tablespoon vegetable oil, divided
1 large egg, beaten
2 tablespoons salted butter, melted
1 teaspoon vanilla extract
1 tablespoon granulated sugar
1 cup whole milk
1½ cups all-purpose flour
1 teaspoon baking powder
¼ teaspoon salt
½ cup confectioners' sugar
2 cups canned whipped cream
4 tablespoons strawberry syrup

1. Heat 48 ounces oil in a large pot over medium heat until it reaches 365°F. Line a large plate with paper towels and set aside.
2. In a large bowl, mix together remaining 1 tablespoon oil, egg, butter, vanilla, granulated sugar, milk, flour, baking powder, and salt.
3. Dip a small cookie scoop into hot oil, then scoop batter and carefully drop into hot oil. Continue adding scoops until pot is half-full. Fry 2–3 minutes until golden brown, turning frequently, then remove to paper towel–lined plate. Repeat with remaining batter.
4. Serve Funnel Puffs immediately on a clean plate, dusted with confectioners' sugar and topped with whipped cream and drizzles of strawberry syrup.

SIGNATURE KEY LIME CHEESECAKE

Thunder Falls Terrace, Islands of Adventure

When visiting Jurassic Park at Islands of Adventure, don't skip VelociCoaster! Dubbed the "apex predator of coasters," VelociCoaster puts you through the paces with two accelerated launches, four inversions, and a 140-foot near-vertical drop. You'll have bragging rights forever if you brave it! Making this citrusy cheesecake takes no bravery whatsoever and can be achieved by the most novice of bakers. Feel free to omit the chocolate curls.

YIELDS 1 (9") CHEESECAKE

FOR CHEESECAKE
- 15 Oreo cookies
- 6 tablespoons salted butter, melted
- 24 ounces cream cheese, softened
- 1 cup granulated sugar
- 1 tablespoon cornstarch
- 3 large eggs
- ⅔ cup key lime juice
- 1 cup canned whipped cream

1. To make Cheesecake: Preheat oven to 300°F and grease a 9" circular springform pan with nonstick cooking spray and set aside.
2. Place Oreo cookies in a food processor or blender and pulse several times until cookies resemble fine crumbs, about 1 minute. Add in melted butter and pulse again several times to combine. Scoop mixture into prepared pan and press firmly across bottom of pan with a greased spatula. Set aside.
3. In the bowl of a stand mixer fitted with a paddle attachment, mix cream cheese, sugar, and cornstarch until well combined, about 2 minutes. Add in eggs one at a time while mixing until combined. Add lime juice and mix an additional 2 minutes. Pour into springform pan over crust.
4. Bake 55–65 minutes or until set. Turn off oven and crack oven door open, but don't remove cheesecake. Allow to sit in open oven 30 minutes.

(continued on next page)

FOR CHOCOLATE CURLS
1 cup dark chocolate chips
1 cup white chocolate chips

5. Remove from oven and chill in refrigerator 6 hours up to overnight.

6. To make Chocolate Curls: Add dark and white chocolate chips to separate small microwave-safe bowls and microwave each 30 seconds, stir, then repeat until chocolate chips just melt.

7. Working quickly, use an offset spatula to spread white chocolate in a thin layer, about 4" × 8", on a clean countertop. Use a chocolate comb to scrape white chocolate into a striped pattern. Allow to set, 5–10 minutes.

8. Pour dark chocolate onto end of white chocolate and spread with offset spatula over white stripes to fill in blank spots made by chocolate comb. Allow dark chocolate to set, 5–10 more minutes. Using a bench scraper, scrape and curl chocolate 1" at a time into long, thin tubes, creating eight striped Chocolate Curls.

9. Pop open springform pan and lift off pan sides and slide off pan bottom. Place cake onto a serving plate. To serve, cut Cheesecake into eight slices and top each slice with 2 tablespoons whipped cream and a Chocolate Curl.

WATURI FUSION ICE CREAM

Koka Poroka, Volcano Bay

....

In all your geographic studies at school, you may have never heard of the Waturi people. That's because they are the fictional group who searched far and wide to find a beautiful place where they could spend quality time with their families— and discovered Volcano Bay! Now the Waturi share their wonderful island with all the guests of Universal Orlando Resort and offer this incredible and unique ice cream treat to keep visitors cool and satiated. Whether at Volcano Bay or at home, do as the Waturi do and set your cares aside for a relaxing and worry-free time with this dish!

SERVES 2

2 cups heavy whipping cream
1 can sweetened condensed milk
¼ teaspoon raspberry extract
2 drops blue gel food coloring
¼ teaspoon banana extract
2 drops yellow gel food coloring
¼ teaspoon orange extract
2 drops orange gel food coloring
¼ teaspoon strawberry extract
2 drops red gel food coloring
2 large waffle cones

1. Whisk together whipping cream and sweetened condensed milk in a large bowl. Pour into an ice cream machine and run according to manufacturer's instructions 15–20 minutes or until thick and creamy. Split evenly into four bowls.

2. To one bowl, add raspberry extract and blue food coloring and mix. To second bowl, add banana extract and yellow food coloring and mix. To third bowl, add orange extract and orange food coloring and mix. To fourth bowl, add strawberry extract and red food coloring and mix. Freeze bowls until ice cream is set, 2–4 hours.

3. Scoop ½ of ice cream from each bowl into 1 waffle cone, piling one scoop on top of the other. Repeat with remaining ingredients. Enjoy immediately.

SIMPLIFICATION HACK

If you don't want to make four flavors of ice cream in one day, don't feel like you have to. Pick and choose which flavors you want to make and go from there. Your Waturi Fusion is yours to decide!

CHOCOLATE LAVA CAKES

Kohola Reef, Volcano Bay

....

Life at Volcano Bay revolves around the massive center volcano, called Krakatau. Honorary Waturi (residents of Volcano Bay) can even board canoes and ride the thrilling Krakatau Aqua Coaster that winds its way down and *up* through the volcano. What better way to celebrate such a feat than diving into a Chocolate Lava Cake? At home, celebrate any of life's achievements with a Chocolate Lava Cake! Got through a tough day? Chocolate Lava Cake! Promotion at work? Chocolate Lava Cake! The Waturi would approve!

SERVES 10

½ cup salted butter, cubed
1 cup bittersweet chocolate chips
2 large eggs
2 large egg yolks
¼ cup granulated sugar
½ teaspoon salt
2 tablespoons all-purpose flour
1¼ cups strawberry syrup
10 teaspoons confectioners' sugar

1. Preheat oven to 450°F. Place ten silicone muffin cups in a standard muffin tin and grease each with nonstick cooking spray. Set aside.
2. In a medium microwave-safe bowl, add butter and chocolate chips. Microwave 30 seconds, stir, then 30 seconds more, and stir again. Repeat until chocolate is melted and smooth.
3. In the bowl of a stand mixer fitted with a whisk attachment, beat eggs, egg yolks, sugar, salt, and flour until light, about 2 minutes. Fold egg mixture into chocolate mixture until uniform.
4. Spoon mixture into prepared muffin cups and bake 8–9 minutes until sides are browning but insides of cakes are still moist.
5. Carefully remove muffin cups from tin while still hot and invert onto individual plates, removing silicone muffin cups. Drizzle each cake with ⅛ cup strawberry syrup and 1 teaspoon sifted confectioners' sugar. Serve immediately.

MACADAMIA NUT COOKIES

Bambu, Volcano Bay

....

Macadamia nuts are some of the most expensive nuts you can buy, and that's in part because they are mostly grown in tropical climates and must be imported around the world. However, the cost is also due to the difficulty in removing their shells. It requires 2,000 newtons of pressure to crack the shell, which is similar in strength to aluminum. That's one tough nut to crack! The resulting interior is a buttery seed with a unique texture. You may want to make an extra batch, since these cookies are sure to get gobbled up quickly!

YIELDS 1 DOZEN COOKIES

½ cup salted butter, softened
⅓ cup light brown sugar
¼ cup granulated sugar
1 large egg
¼ teaspoon vanilla extract
¼ teaspoon almond extract
2½ cups all-purpose flour
½ teaspoon baking soda
½ teaspoon salt
½ cup coarsely chopped salted macadamia nuts
½ cup white chocolate chips

1. Preheat oven to 350°F. Line two baking sheets with parchment paper and set aside.
2. In the bowl of a stand mixer fitted with a paddle attachment, cream together butter, brown sugar, and granulated sugar 2 minutes. Add egg, vanilla, almond extract, flour, baking soda, and salt and mix 2 minutes. Fold in macadamia nuts and white chocolate chips until combined.
3. Using an extra-large cookie scoop (about 3 table-spoons), scoop dough onto prepared baking sheets, leaving about 3" between scoops.
4. Bake one sheet at a time 15–20 minutes or until cookies are golden brown. Allow cookies to cool on sheets about 10 minutes, then serve. Leftover cookies can be stored in an airtight container at room temperature up to 1 week.

UNICORN CUPCAKES

Minion Cafe, Universal Studios Hollywood

In the movie *Despicable Me*, the littlest of the three orphans, Agnes, is obsessed with unicorns. It is seen as a huge turning point for Gru's character when he wins a carnival game to get Agnes a unicorn. Thus, the unicorn theme prevails across the Minion area of Universal Studios Hollywood. This cupcake is delightfully fluffy (just like a unicorn), and the edible glitter really adds that extra magic that a unicorn cupcake deserves.

YIELDS 1½ DOZEN CUPCAKES

FOR CUPCAKES
1 (15.25-ounce) box white cake mix
4 large eggs
1 cup salted butter, melted
1 cup whole milk
¼ cup rainbow sprinkles

FOR BUTTERCREAM FROSTING
1 cup salted butter, softened
3 tablespoons vanilla extract
4 cups confectioners' sugar
2 tablespoons whole milk
2 drops purple gel food coloring
2 drops orange gel food coloring
2 drops yellow gel food coloring
2 drops blue gel food coloring
2 tablespoons edible glitter

1. To make Cupcakes: Preheat oven to 350°F. Line a muffin tin with paper liners and set aside.
2. In a large bowl, mix together cake mix, eggs, butter, and milk. Fold in sprinkles. Scoop batter into paper liners until about ⅔ full, reserving extra batter.
3. Bake 13–17 minutes until a knife inserted in center comes out clean.
4. Remove from oven, remove cupcakes to a wire rack, re-line muffin tin, and repeat filling and baking with remaining batter. Allow cupcakes to cool completely before frosting, about 1 hour.
5. To make Buttercream Frosting: In the bowl of a stand mixer fitted with a whisk attachment, cream butter and vanilla until smooth, about 2 minutes. Add confectioners' sugar and milk and mix until well combined, about 2 minutes. Divide frosting evenly into four bowls and color one purple, one orange, one yellow, and one blue with gel food coloring.
6. Scoop each color into a small piping bag and gather all four piping bags into one large piping bag fitted with a star tip. Swirl colors out of star tip in a conical pattern on each cupcake. Finish with a dusting of edible glitter and serve.

NUTELLA BANANA PUDDING

Minion Cafe, Universal Studios Hollywood

During the COVID-19 pandemic, Universal Parks had to close their gates as a safety precaution. While Universal Orlando Resort had a brief closure, Universal Studios Hollywood remained closed for over a year. Clever Universal executives found a way for guests to return to the Park: Turn it into an "outdoor restaurant." Each food location offered special dishes, and all food was to be eaten alfresco. At this event, Minion Cafe was first introduced, and guests fell in love with the Nutella Banana Pudding. Delicious and super *Instagram*mable, what's not to love?!

SERVES 6

1 (3.9-ounce) box instant chocolate pudding mix
4 cups whole milk, divided
1 (3.4-ounce) box instant banana cream pudding mix
¼ cup hazelnut spread
3 cups canned whipped cream
12 tablespoons yellow fondant
8 tablespoons gray fondant
6 tablespoons white fondant
5 tablespoons black fondant

1. Prepare chocolate pudding by whisking chocolate pudding mix and 2 cups milk in a medium bowl. Set in refrigerator 10 minutes. Prepare banana cream pudding by whisking banana cream pudding mix and remaining 2 cups milk in another medium bowl. Set in refrigerator 10 minutes.

2. Once chocolate pudding is set, stir hazelnut spread into pudding. Scoop ¼ cup chocolate-hazelnut pudding into the bottoms of six clear plastic teacups. Scoop ¼ cup banana cream pudding on top of each chocolate-hazelnut pudding layer. Top each with ½ cup whipped cream and smooth out into a level surface.

3. Using colored fondants, make a Minion design: One 3" yellow circle, topped by one 1¼" gray circle, one 1" white circle, and one ½" black circle. Add two black strips to the sides of the gray circle as the "goggle strap." Place on top of whipped cream and repeat for remaining cups. Serve.

BIRTHDAY CAKE DOUGH BITES

Super Silly Stuff, Universal Studios Hollywood

You don't need to wait for a birthday to make a batch of these *Despicable Me*-inspired treats—it's always *someone's* birthday *somewhere*, right? Make any day a celebration with these little bites of joy. These are served prepackaged at Universal in a pink box adorned with Agnes's favorite unicorn. Eat in a bag, in a bowl, or on a plate; however you want them is up to you.

YIELDS 3-4 DOZEN BITES

½ cup salted butter, softened
⅔ cup granulated sugar
⅓ cup light brown sugar
1 teaspoon vanilla extract
1 cup cake flour
¼ teaspoon baking soda
¼ teaspoon salt
1 tablespoon heavy whipping
 cream
2 cups white chocolate chips
1 teaspoon coconut oil
1 teaspoon blue crystal
 sprinkles
1 teaspoon yellow crystal
 sprinkles
1 teaspoon pink crystal
 sprinkles

1. Grease a baking sheet with nonstick cooking spray and set aside. In the bowl of a stand mixer fitted with a paddle attachment, cream together butter, granulated sugar, and brown sugar until soft. Add in vanilla, flour, baking soda, and salt and mix. Drizzle in cream while mixing to get dough to a non-crumbly texture that will hold a ball shape.
2. Roll ½ teaspoon dough into a ball and place on prepared baking sheet. Repeat with remaining dough. Place sheet in refrigerator to set about 2 hours.
3. Once dough is set, prepare coating: Place white chocolate chips and coconut oil in a small microwave-safe bowl and microwave 30 seconds, stir, then microwave 30 seconds more and stir again. Repeat until chips just melt.
4. Mix sprinkle colors together in a separate small bowl and sprinkle into white chocolate. Use a fork to dip dough balls into chocolate one at a time and place back on greased baking sheet. Once all balls are coated, return to refrigerator to set 1 hour. Serve.

CHAPTER 8

DRINKS

Beverages are such a fun way to create a bit of movie magic very easily in your home. Requiring few ingredients and no specialty equipment beyond a blender, truly anyone can make the drinks enjoyed by Universal Parkgoers.

In this chapter, you'll find popular beverages from the four US Universal Parks. And anyone can partake in these drinks! All recipes ahead are 100 percent alcohol-free so that every member of the family can have a sip. Including favorites like Pumpkin Juice, the Flaming Moe, and Moose Juice, as well as adventurous concoctions like the Amphorae Shrub and more indulgent options like Felonious Floats, there is something to satisfy everyone's tastes. You'll be sipping away in just minutes with these easy recipes! The hardest part will be choosing what drink to start with.

FISHY GREEN ALE

The Hopping Pot, Universal Studios Florida

This drink looks fishy. Like, really fishy—from the interesting color and pearls
on the bottom of the cup. But rest assured that it doesn't *taste* fishy. It has a
unique yet incredibly delicious flavor. You'd never think that cinnamon, mint,
and blueberry could possibly belong in the same cup, but somehow it *works*.
Universal chefs created something special in this drink, and now
you can enjoy it whenever you want right at home.

SERVES 1

FOR SYRUP
½ cup water
½ cup granulated sugar
3 cinnamon sticks
½ teaspoon mint extract

FOR ALE
½ cup blueberry popping
   pearls
9 ounces chilled club soda
¼ teaspoon half-and-half
1 drop green liquid food
   coloring

1. To make Syrup: In a small saucepan over medium
   heat, combine water, sugar, cinnamon sticks, and
   mint extract. Stir frequently until mixture comes to
   a boil, then remove from heat. Allow to cool to room
   temperature, about 1 hour, then strain into a small bowl
   or jar.

2. To make Ale: Pour blueberry popping pearls into a
   16-ounce glass or plastic cup, followed by club soda,
   3 ounces Syrup, half-and-half, and food coloring. Stir to
   combine and serve immediately. Leftover Syrup can be
   kept in an airtight container in refrigerator up to 4 days.

FIRE PROTECTION POTION

Eternelle's Elixir of Refreshment, Universal Studios Florida

As told in the Harry Potter book series, witches who were being burned at the stake during medieval inquisitions would cast fire protection spells upon themselves so as not to suffer death by fire. Eternelle's wanted to make this spell easier (and tastier) by concocting a potion that could be mixed with water and drunk. If you're having a party, make the recipe in bulk and portion into small vials that party guests can pour into their own bottles of water.

SERVES 1

¼ cup granulated sugar
¼ teaspoon watermelon
  Kool-Aid drink mix
1 ounce water

1. Mix together sugar, Kool-Aid drink mix, and water in a small microwave-safe bowl. Microwave 1 minute, stir, then microwave 1 minute more. Stir and allow to cool completely at room temperature, about 1 hour.
2. When ready to enjoy, pour into a 16.9-ounce bottle of water, cap, and shake to combine.

 **MIX IT UP**

Eternelle's sells many different flavors of potions that tout unique spells, including Babbling Beverage, Draught of Peace, and Elixir to Induce Euphoria. Sub in a different flavor of Kool-Aid drink mix to make other potions!

GROOVY GROVE JUICE

Moe's Tavern, Universal Studios Florida

In *The Simpsons* series, Groovy Grove Juice is a corporation that makes and bottles vegetable juice from a farm that used to be a hippie commune in the 1960s. Its juice is called Garden Blast and is packed full of organic vegetables. Universal chefs must have decided that most people visiting the Parks would rather wet their whistles with a fruit juice instead of a vegetable juice and made it a refreshing orange and lemonade frozen beverage.

SERVES 1

FOR LEMONADE KOOL-AID SYRUP
1 (0.16-ounce) packet lemonade Kool-Aid drink mix
1 cup granulated sugar
1 cup water

FOR JUICE
2 ounces blood orange syrup
2 ounces pulp-free orange juice
3 cups crushed ice

1. To make Lemonade Kool-Aid Syrup: Combine all ingredients in a small saucepan over medium-high heat and bring to a boil. Once boiling, remove from heat and allow to cool to room temperature, about 1 hour.
2. Pour Syrup into a medium sealable container and chill at least 1 hour, up to 4 weeks.
3. To make Juice: In a blender, add 6 ounces Lemonade Kool-Aid Syrup, blood orange syrup, orange juice, and crushed ice. Blend until smooth. Pour into a large plastic cup or glass and serve immediately.

FLAMING MOE

Moe's Tavern, Universal Studios Florida

In season three of *The Simpsons*, Homer tells the bartender Moe about a bizarre mixed drink he made at home, which combined several spirits with children's cough syrup, and then lit on fire. He called it the "Flaming Homer" and made one for Moe. Moe loved it and commandeered it for himself, naming it the "Flaming Moe." While the drink in the TV show is distinctly purple, Universal decided to make their Flaming Moe an orange-red. No alcohol (or cough syrup!) is included, so everyone can enjoy this special concoction.

SERVES 1

2 cups orange soda
½ cup fruit punch

Pour all ingredients into a short (8–10 ounce) glass or plastic cup and stir gently to combine.

COOKING TIP

Universal makes this drink "flaming" by adding dry ice. They engineered a special cup that has a chamber on the bottom that holds the dry ice and keeps it away from the drinker's mouth. Don't try this at home—dry ice can stick to your lips and cause burns!

MR. TEENY

Moe's Tavern, Universal Studios Florida

Mr. Teeny is the ape sidekick of Krusty the Clown from *The Simpsons*. He originally hails from Brazil, and as such this drink is distinctly tropical to honor his heritage. Delicious lemonade, blue curaçao, and pineapple flavors blend beautifully. Mix one up to keep you cool on a warm day!

SERVES 2

FOR LEMONADE KOOL-AID SYRUP
- 1 (0.16-ounce) packet lemonade Kool-Aid drink mix
- 1 cup granulated sugar
- 1 cup water

FOR ASSEMBLY
- 1 ounce blue curaçao syrup
- 2 ounces pineapple juice
- 3 cups crushed ice

1. To make Lemonade Kool-Aid Syrup: Combine all ingredients in a small saucepan over medium-high heat and bring to a boil. Once boiling, remove from heat and allow to cool to room temperature, about 1 hour.
2. Pour Syrup into a medium sealable container and chill at least 1 hour, up to 4 weeks.
3. To Assemble: Add 7 ounces Lemonade Kool-Aid Syrup to a blender along with blue curaçao syrup, pineapple juice, and crushed ice. Blend until smooth and pour into two plastic cups or glasses. Serve.

THE FRISCO SHAKE, VANILLA

Richter's Burger Co., Universal Studios Florida

....

Richter's Burger Co. is named after the scientific scale used to rate the severity of earthquakes: the Richter scale. As such, many items on the menu allude to earthquakes, like The Big One, The Aftershock, and The Frisco Shake (San Francisco being an earthquake hot spot). The Park used to have an attraction called Disaster!, which brought guests right into the middle of a film set featuring a massive earthquake. While this attraction closed in 2015 to make way for Fast & Furious–Supercharged, guests can still eat at Richter's Burger Co. and sip on a creamy vanilla Frisco Shake to cool down on a hot Florida day.

SERVES 1

3 cups vanilla ice cream
¼ cup whole milk

Add vanilla ice cream and milk to a blender and blend until smooth. Pour into a large plastic cup or glass and serve immediately with a straw.

 **MIX IT UP**

The Frisco Shake is also available in chocolate at Richter's Burger Co., so if you want to mix things up with this recipe, simply swap the vanilla ice cream for chocolate ice cream instead.

MOOSE JUICE

Moose Juice, Goose Juice, Islands of Adventure

Moose Juice and Goose Juice are mentioned in *Dr. Seuss's Sleep Book*, where he warns the moose not to drink goose juice and warns the goose not to drink moose juice. Mostly it is a silly tongue twister that makes no sense, but at Universal (and now at home), Moose Juice and Goose Juice are real, and you can choose which one you'd rather sip on—or enjoy both!

SERVES 1

FOR ORANGE KOOL-AID SYRUP
1 (0.16-ounce) packet orange Kool-Aid drink mix
1 cup granulated sugar
1 cup water

FOR JUICE
2 ounces club soda
3 cups crushed ice

1. To make Orange Kool-Aid Syrup: Combine all ingredients in a small saucepan over medium-high heat and bring to a boil. Once boiling, remove from heat and allow to cool to room temperature, about 1 hour.
2. Pour Syrup into a medium sealable container and chill at least 1 hour, up to 4 weeks.
3. To make Juice: Add 8 ounces Orange Kool-Aid Syrup to a blender with club soda and crushed ice. Blend until smooth and pour into a 16-ounce glass or plastic cup. Serve.

GOOSE JUICE

Moose Juice, Goose Juice, Islands of Adventure

Seuss Landing is a great place for kids to play at Islands of Adventure. You are even allowed to bring food and drinks into the play areas so you can munch while you play, and that includes this yummy green apple Goose Juice. Next time you take your kids to the local playground, pack up some Goose Juice in a travel bottle and simulate the experience of Universal in your own town!

SERVES 1

FOR GREEN APPLE KOOL-AID SYRUP
1 (0.16-ounce) packet green apple Kool-Aid drink mix
1 cup granulated sugar
1 cup water

FOR JUICE
2 ounces club soda
3 cups crushed ice

1. To make Green Apple Kool-Aid Syrup: Combine all ingredients in a small saucepan over medium-high heat and bring to a boil. Once boiling, remove from heat and allow to cool to room temperature, about 1 hour.
2. Pour Syrup into a medium sealable container and chill at least 1 hour, up to 4 weeks.
3. To make Juice: Add 8 ounces Green Apple Kool-Aid Syrup to a blender with club soda and crushed ice. Blend until smooth and pour into a 16-ounce glass or plastic cup. Serve.

AMPHORAE SHRUB

Mythos Restaurant, Islands of Adventure

....

This drink may sound like it is firmly rooted in the ground—but it isn't that kind of shrub! A drink "shrub" is a syrup made with fruits, sugars, and vinegar that is mixed with water to form a refreshing and tart beverage. Shrubs have been around a long time (just like the gods and goddesses of Mythos Restaurant) and were originally used as a form of preserving fruit, since the vinegar and bottling process keep the shrub fresh for about 6 months. You'll instantly feel transported to ancient Greece as you sip this unique drink.

SERVES 6

1 cup granulated sugar
1 cup white wine vinegar
⅓ cup fresh blueberries
⅓ cup fresh raspberries
⅓ cup fresh blackberries
Zest of 1 lime
½ teaspoon mint extract
6¾ cups club soda
6 lemon wedges

1. Add sugar, vinegar, blueberries, raspberries, blackberries, lime zest, and mint extract to a small saucepan over medium heat. Mash ingredients with a potato masher until well smashed, and stir until mixture starts to boil, 3–5 minutes. Pour contents of saucepan into a bowl or jar, cover, and refrigerate 4 hours up to overnight.

2. When ready to serve, strain 2 ounces berry mixture each into six drinking glasses. Add club soda and fill remainder of glasses with ice. Place 1 lemon wedge on rim of each glass and enjoy.

PUMPKIN JUICE

Hog's Head, Islands of Adventure

Referenced in the Harry Potter books and movies, Pumpkin Juice is served as a fresh, on-tap beverage at dining locations or can be found bottled in coolers and carts across The Wizarding World. The bottles are handy because they can be thrown in a bag for later and have an adorable pumpkin lid that makes a cute souvenir. This light and fresh drink is perfect for a hot day.

SERVES 1

1½ cups cold spiced apple cider
1 ounce pumpkin spice syrup

Add all ingredients to a cocktail shaker half-full of ice.
Shake and strain into a large plastic cup or glass.
Top with more ice and enjoy.

BERRY BLAST

Dancing Dragons Boat Bar, Volcano Bay

....

Whether you're visiting Volcano Bay or spending a day at home, this yummy slush is the perfect fruity pick-me-up. It's served in a large glass and topped with strawberry slices; grab two straws and share with a friend! Dancing Dragons Boat Bar serves several flavors of this slush, including mango and piña colada. Change up the juices and fruits in this recipe to try out different blends! Complete the tropical vibes with a colorful drink umbrella.

SERVES 1

4 ounces apple juice
½ ounce lime juice
⅓ cup frozen strawberries
⅓ cup frozen raspberries
⅓ cup frozen blueberries
1 ounce simple syrup
1 fresh strawberry, hulled
  and sliced

Add apple juice, lime juice, frozen strawberries, frozen raspberries, frozen blueberries, and simple syrup to a blender and blend until smooth. Pour into a 16-ounce plastic cup or glass, top with sliced strawberry, and serve with a straw.

FELONIOUS FLOATS

Minion Cafe, Universal Studios Hollywood

Some people forget that *Despicable Me* begins with the premise of two supervillains who are trying to out-bad each other and do the most dastardly deeds. "Felonious" means something related to a crime, and with the incorporation of the Minion-beloved banana, the Felonious Floats work perfectly at Minion Cafe.

SERVES 4

FOR BANANA SOFT SERVE
2 cups whole milk
½ cup granulated sugar
½ cup heavy whipping cream
½ teaspoon banana extract
¼ teaspoon salt
4 drops yellow gel food coloring

FOR BLUE RASPBERRY KOOL-AID SYRUP
1 (0.16-ounce) packet blue raspberry Kool-Aid drink mix
1 cup granulated sugar
1 cup water

FOR BLUE RASPBERRY SLUSHY
2 ounces club soda
3 cups crushed ice

FOR ASSEMBLY
2 cups canned whipped cream
4 teaspoons blue sugar sprinkles
4 tablespoons banana candies

1. To make Banana Soft Serve: Blend all ingredients in a blender until well combined. Pour into an ice cream machine and run according to manufacturer's instructions about 15 minutes or until creamy. Scoop into a medium freezer-safe container, cover, and place in freezer until ready to use, up to 4 days.

2. To make Blue Raspberry Kool-Aid Syrup: Combine all ingredients in a small saucepan over medium-high heat and bring to a boil. Once boiling, remove from heat and allow to cool to room temperature, about 1 hour.

3. Pour Syrup into a medium sealable container and chill at least 1 hour, up to 4 weeks.

4. To make Blue Raspberry Slushy: In a clean blender, add 8 ounces Blue Raspberry Kool-Aid Syrup, club soda, and crushed ice. Blend until smooth.

5. To Assemble: Divide half of Blue Raspberry Slushy evenly among four 18-ounce glasses or plastic cups. Scoop Banana Soft Serve into cups. Layer with remaining Blue Raspberry Slushy. Top each glass with ½ cup whipped cream, 1 teaspoon blue sugar sprinkles, and 1 tablespoon banana candies. Serve immediately.

TIKI TAI

Isla Nu-Bar, Universal Studios Hollywood

Isla Nu-Bar is an ultra-popular location at Universal Studios Hollywood, so be sure to schedule time to wait in line if you're hoping for a Tiki Tai on your Park day. Each drink is prepared fresh in front of you, so the line can move slowly. Luckily, this drink is super easy to make at home and you'll never have to wait in line at your own refrigerator. Orgeat can be found at specialty stores or from online retailers. Garnish with an orchid flower to complete the tropical feel.

SERVES 1

6 ounces pineapple juice
1½ ounces lime juice
1½ ounces orgeat
3 ounces club soda

Add pineapple juice, lime juice, and orgeat to a cocktail shaker half-full of ice. Shake well and pour into a tiki glass. Add fresh ice almost to fill and top with club soda. Serve.

DUFF A L'ORANGE
SPARKLING BEVERAGE

Kwik-E-Mart, Universal Studios Hollywood

Duff is famously a beer brand seen on *The Simpsons*, but Universal wanted young and old alike to be able to enjoy a can of Duff, so they made it a diet sparkling orange drink. Multiply this recipe and share with family or friends. If you'd like an "actual" Duff Beer, just head over to Duff Brewery Beer Garden, where they have Duff Beer available on draft.

SERVES 1

¾ teaspoon orange drink enhancer

11 ounces sparkling water, chilled

Gently stir orange drink enhancer into sparkling water in a large plastic cup or glass until well combined. Serve immediately.

UNIVERSAL THEME PARKS MAPS

Use the following maps to discover where you can find each of the recipes in Part 2 in the four main Universal Theme Parks locations: Universal Studios Florida, Universal's Islands of Adventure, Universal's Volcano Bay, and Universal Studios Hollywood. Each map includes a numbered key, so you can match a numbered circle on that map to what dish or drink is found there, as well as what chapter of this book the recipe for that treat can be found in.

UNIVERSAL STUDIOS FLORIDA

NEW YORK

13

PRODUCTION CENTRAL

Schwab's PHARMACY

30

11

5

TODAY Café

1 **2** **3** **4**

9

HOLLYWOOD

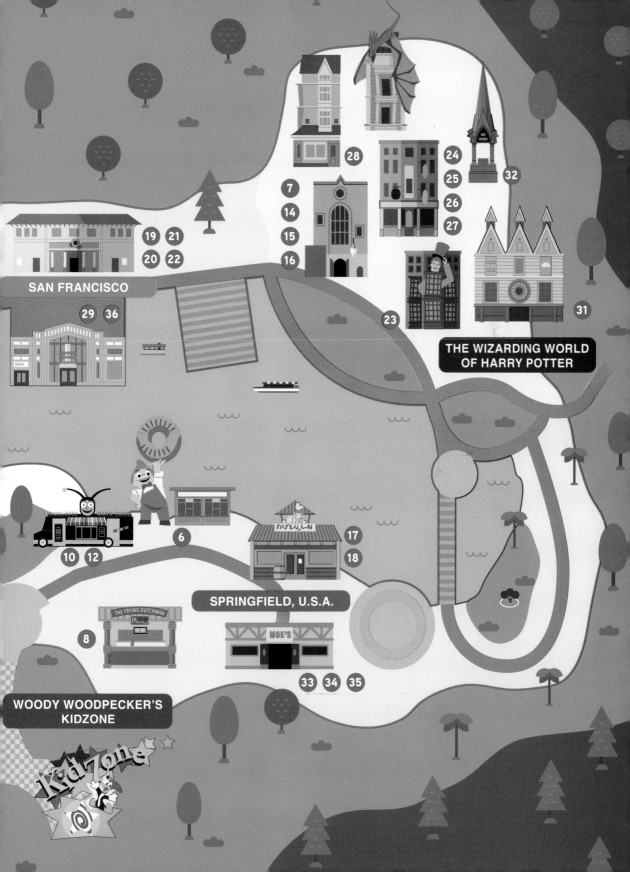

UNIVERSAL STUDIOS FLORIDA

1. **EGG WHITE FLORENTINE** (*Today* Cafe, USF, Chapter 3: Breakfasts and Pastries)

2. **CINNAMON SUGAR CRUFFINS** (*Today* Cafe, USF, Chapter 3: Breakfasts and Pastries)

3. **OVERNIGHT OATS** (*Today* Cafe, USF, Chapter 3: Breakfasts and Pastries)

4. **VEGAN ELDERBERRY CROISSANTS** (*Today* Cafe, USF, Chapter 3: Breakfasts and Pastries)

5. **RASPBERRY AND PASSION FRUIT CREAM CREPES** (Central Park Crêpes, USF, Chapter 3: Breakfasts and Pastries)

6. **THE BIG PINK** (Lard Lad Donuts, USF, SIMPSONS, Chapter 3: Breakfasts and Pastries)

7. **SCOTCH EGGS** (Leaky Cauldron, USF, HARRY POTTER, Chapter 4: Appetizers and Snacks)

8. **CLAM CHOWD-ARR** (The Frying Dutchman, USF, SIMPSONS, Chapter 4: Appetizers and Snacks)

9. **PIZZA-STUFFED PRETZELS** (Carmen's Veranda, USF, Chapter 4: Appetizers and Snacks)

10. **KOREAN BEEF TACOS** (Bumblebee Man's Taco Truck, USF, SIMPSONS, Chapter 4: Appetizers and Snacks)

11. **SMOKED BRISKET CREPES** (Central Park Crêpes, USF, Chapter 4: Appetizers and Snacks)

12. **CARNE ASADA TACOS** (Bumblebee Man's Taco Truck, USF, SIMPSONS, Chapter 4: Appetizers and Snacks)

13. **FINNEGAN'S POTATO AND ONION WEBBS** (Finnegan's Bar & Grill, USF, Chapter 4: Appetizers and Snacks)

14. **FISHERMAN'S PIE** (Leaky Cauldron, USF, HARRY POTTER, Chapter 5: Entrées)

15. **COTTAGE PIE** (Leaky Cauldron, USF, HARRY POTTER, Chapter 5: Entrées)

16. **BEEF, LAMB, AND GUINNESS STEW** (Leaky Cauldron, USF, HARRY POTTER, Chapter 5: Entrées)

17. **CHICKEN THUMBS** (Cletus' Chicken Shack, USF, SIMPSONS, Chapter 5: Entrées)

18. **CHICKEN AND WAFFLE SANDWICHES** (Cletus' Chicken Shack, USF, SIMPSONS, Chapter 5: Entrées)

19. **MINION APPLES** (San Francisco Candy Factory, USF, MINIONS, Chapter 6: Sugar Confections)

20. **BUTTER PECAN FUDGE** (San Francisco Candy Factory, USF, Chapter 6: Sugar Confections)

21. **BLUE CAMO FUDGE** (San Francisco Candy Factory, USF, JURASSIC PARK, Chapter 6: Sugar Confections)

22. **MILK CHOCOLATE PECAN PATTIES** (San Francisco Candy Factory, USF, JURASSIC PARK, Chapter 6: Sugar Confections)

23. **LOVE POTION** (Weasleys' Wizard Wheezes, USF, HARRY POTTER, Chapter 6: Sugar Confections)

24. **FAINTING FANCIES** (Weasleys' Wizard Wheezes, USF, HARRY POTTER, Chapter 6: Sugar Confections)

25 NOSEBLEED NOUGAT (Weasleys' Wizard Wheezes, USF, HARRY POTTER, Chapter 6: Sugar Confections)

26 FEVER FUDGE (Weasleys' Wizard Wheezes, USF, HARRY POTTER, Chapter 6: Sugar Confections)

27 PUKING PASTILLES (Weasleys' Wizard Wheezes, USF, HARRY POTTER, Chapter 6: Sugar Confections)

28 STRAWBERRY AND PEANUT BUTTER ICE CREAM (Florean Fortescue's Ice Cream Parlor, USF, HARRY POTTER, Chapter 7: Desserts)

29 MILE HIGH APPLE PIE (Richter's Burger Co., USF, Chapter 7: Desserts)

30 PINEAPPLE DOLE WHIP (Schwab's Pharmacy, USF, Chapter 7: Desserts)

31 FISHY GREEN ALE (The Hopping Pot, USF, HARRY POTTER, Chapter 8: Drinks)

32 FIRE PROTECTION POTION (Eternelle's Elixir of Refreshment, USF, HARRY POTTER, Chapter 8: Drinks)

33 GROOVY GROVE JUICE (Moe's Tavern, USF, SIMPSONS, Chapter 8: Drinks)

34 FLAMING MOE (Moe's Tavern, USF, SIMPSONS, Chapter 8: Drinks)

35 MR. TEENY (Moe's Tavern, USF, SIMPSONS, Chapter 8: Drinks)

36 THE FRISCO SHAKE, VANILLA (Richter's Burger Co., USF, Chapter 8: Drinks)

UNIVERSAL'S VOLCANO BAY

37 JERK SHRIMP MAC AND CHEESE (Whakawaiwai Eats, UVB, Chapter 4: Appetizers and Snacks)

38 ISLAND CHICKEN SALAD (Whakawaiwai Eats, UVB, Chapter 4: Appetizers and Snacks)

39 COCONUT-CRUSTED FRIED CHICKEN (Kohola Reef, UVB, Chapter 5: Entrées)

40 JERKED MAHI SANDWICHES (Kohola Reef, UVB, Chapter 5: Entrées)

41 COCONUT CURRY CHICKEN (Kohola Reef, UVB, Chapter 5: Entrées)

42 MANGO BBQ PULLED PORK SANDWICHES (Kohola Reef, UVB, Chapter 5: Entrées)

43 WATURI FUSION ICE CREAM (Koka Poroka, UVB, Chapter 7: Desserts)

44 CHOCOLATE LAVA CAKES (Kohola Reef, UVB, Chapter 7: Desserts)

45 MACADAMIA NUT COOKIES (Bambu, UVB, Chapter 7: Desserts)

46 BERRY BLAST (Dancing Dragons Boat Bar, UVB, Chapter 8: Drinks)

UNIVERSAL'S VOLCANO BAY

WAVE VILLAGE

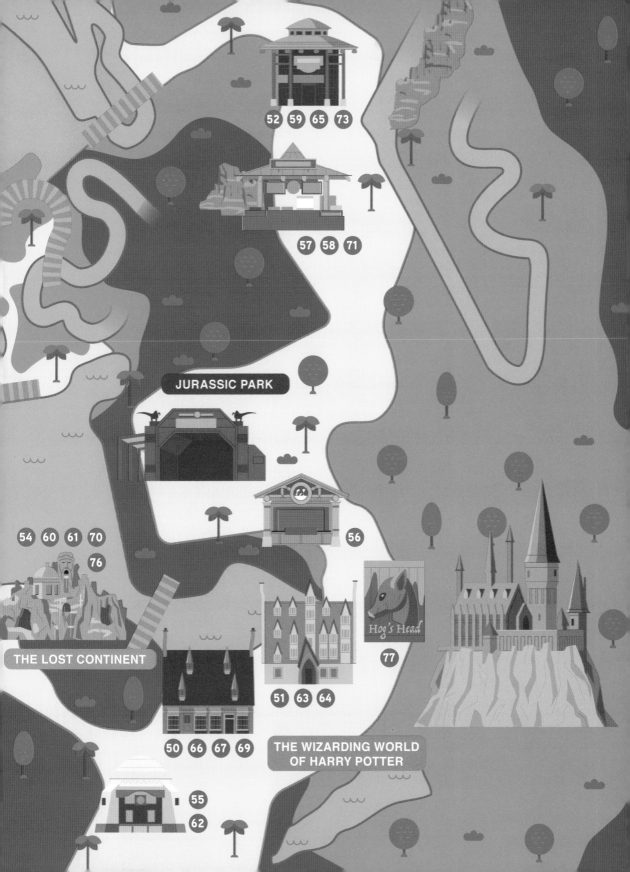

52 59 65 73

57 58 71

JURASSIC PARK

54 60 61 70 76

56

THE LOST CONTINENT

Hog's Head

77

51 63 64

50 66 67 69

THE WIZARDING WORLD
OF HARRY POTTER

55

62

UNIVERSAL'S ISLANDS OF ADVENTURE

47 HAM, EGG, AND CHEESE EMPANADAS (Croissant Moon Bakery, UIOA, Chapter 3: Breakfasts and Pastries)

48 STRAWBERRY AND CHEESE POP TARTS (Croissant Moon Bakery, UIOA, Chapter 3: Breakfasts and Pastries)

49 GREEN EGGS AND HAM TOTS (Green Eggs and Ham Cafe, UIOA, DR. SEUSS, Chapter 3: Breakfasts and Pastries)

50 PUMPKIN PASTIES (Honeydukes, UIOA, HARRY POTTER, Chapter 3: Breakfasts and Pastries)

51 CHILD TRADITIONAL ENGLISH BREAKFAST (Three Broomsticks, UIOA, HARRY POTTER, Chapter 3: Breakfasts and Pastries)

52 BANANA CREME TARTS (Thunder Falls Terrace, UIOA, JURASSIC PARK, Chapter 3: Breakfasts and Pastries)

53 WHO HASH (Green Eggs and Ham Cafe, UIOA, DR. SEUSS, Chapter 4: Appetizers and Snacks)

54 SPANAKOPITA DIP (Mythos Restaurant, UIOA, Chapter 4: Appetizers and Snacks)

55 HUMMUS (Doc Sugrue's Desert Kebab House, UIOA, Chapter 4: Appetizers and Snacks)

56 PULLED PORK NACHOS (The Watering Hole, UIOA, JURASSIC PARK, Chapter 4: Appetizers and Snacks)

57 PAPAS RELLENAS (Natural Selections, UIOA, JURASSIC PARK, Chapter 4: Appetizers and Snacks)

58 BEEF EMPANADAS (Natural Selections, UIOA, JURASSIC PARK, Chapter 4: Appetizers and Snacks)

59 TURKEY LEGS (Thunder Falls Terrace, UIOA, JURASSIC PARK, Chapter 4: Appetizers and Snacks)

60 MYTHOS SIGNATURE LAMB BURGERS (Mythos Restaurant, UIOA, Chapter 5: Entrées)

61 FORK, KNIFE, AND SPOON GRILLED CHEESE (Mythos Restaurant, UIOA, Chapter 5: Entrées)

62 CHICKEN KEBAB (Doc Sugrue's Desert Kebab House, UIOA, Chapter 5: Entrées)

63 FISH AND CHIPS (Three Broomsticks, UIOA, HARRY POTTER, Chapter 5: Entrées)

64 SPARERIBS PLATTER (Three Broomsticks, UIOA, HARRY POTTER, Chapter 5: Entrées)

65 ROASTED PERNIL (Thunder Falls Terrace, UIOA, JURASSIC PARK, Chapter 5: Entrées)

66 NO MELT ICE CREAM (Honeydukes, UIOA, HARRY POTTER, Chapter 6: Sugar Confections)

67 FELIX FELICIS (Honeydukes, UIOA, HARRY POTTER, Chapter 6: Sugar Confections)

68 SUNDAES ON A STICK (Hop on Pop Ice Cream Shop, UIOA, DR. SEUSS, Chapter 7: Desserts)

69 PUMPKIN CAKES (Honeydukes, UIOA, HARRY POTTER, Chapter 7: Desserts)

70 LAVENDER BLUEBERRY PANNA COTTA (Mythos Restaurant, UIOA, Chapter 7: Desserts)

71 **DULCE DE LECHE CHURROS** (Natural Selections, UIOA, JURASSIC PARK, Chapter 7: Desserts)

72 **FUNNEL PUFFS** (Comic Strip Cafe, UIOA, Chapter 7: Desserts)

73 **SIGNATURE KEY LIME CHEESECAKE** (Thunder Falls Terrace, UIOA, JURASSIC PARK, Chapter 7: Desserts)

74 **MOOSE JUICE** (Moose Juice, Goose Juice, UIOA, DR. SEUSS, Chapter 8: Drinks)

75 **GOOSE JUICE** (Moose Juice, Goose Juice, UIOA, DR. SEUSS, Chapter 8: Drinks)

76 **AMPHORAE SHRUB** (Mythos Restaurant, UIOA, Chapter 8: Drinks)

77 **PUMPKIN JUICE** (Hog's Head, UIOA, HARRY POTTER, Chapter 8: Drinks)

UNIVERSAL STUDIOS HOLLYWOOD

78 **LEMON POPPY BUNDTS** (French Street Bistro, USH, Chapter 3: Breakfasts and Pastries)

79 **BEIGNETS** (French Street Bistro, USH, Chapter 3: Breakfasts and Pastries)

80 **VEGETARIAN CORN DOGS** (Mummy Eats, USH, THE MUMMY, Chapter 4: Appetizers and Snacks)

81 **GRILLED ELOTE WITH TAJÍN** (Little Cocina, USH, Chapter 4: Appetizers and Snacks)

82 **KOREAN CORN DOGS** (Mummy Eats, USH, THE MUMMY, Chapter 4: Appetizers and Snacks)

83 **MEATBALL PARMESAN GRILLED CHEESE WITH TOMATO SOUP** (Minion Cafe, USH, MINIONS, Chapter 5: Entrées)

84 **PULLED PORK GRILLED CHEESES WITH BANANA BBQ SAUCE** (Minion Cafe, USH, MINIONS, Chapter 5: Entrées)

85 **SLOW-ROASTED MOJO JACKFRUIT** (Jurassic Cafe, USH, JURASSIC PARK, Chapter 5: Entrées)

86 **KRUSTY BURGER** (Krusty Burger, USH, SIMPSONS, Chapter 5: Entrées)

87 **TROPICAL ROASTED CHICKEN SALAD** (Jurassic Cafe, USH, JURASSIC PARK, Chapter 5: Entrées)

88 **CHOCOLATE AND BANANA COTTON CANDY** (Super Silly Stuff, USH, MINIONS, Chapter 6: Sugar Confections)

89 **SPICED CASHEW BRITTLE** (City Snack Shop, USH, Chapter 6: Sugar Confections)

90 **UNICORN CUPCAKES** (Minion Cafe, USH, MINIONS, Chapter 7: Desserts)

91 **NUTELLA BANANA PUDDING** (Minion Cafe, USH, MINIONS, Chapter 7: Desserts)

92 **BIRTHDAY CAKE DOUGH BITES** (Super Silly Stuff, USH, MINIONS, Chapter 7: Desserts)

93 **FELONIOUS FLOATS** (Minion Cafe, USH, MINIONS, Chapter 8: Drinks)

94 **TIKI TAI** (Isla Nu-Bar, USH, JURASSIC PARK, Chapter 8: Drinks)

95 **DUFF A L'ORANGE SPARKLING BEVERAGE** (Kwik-E-Mart, USH, SIMPSONS, Chapter 8: Drinks)

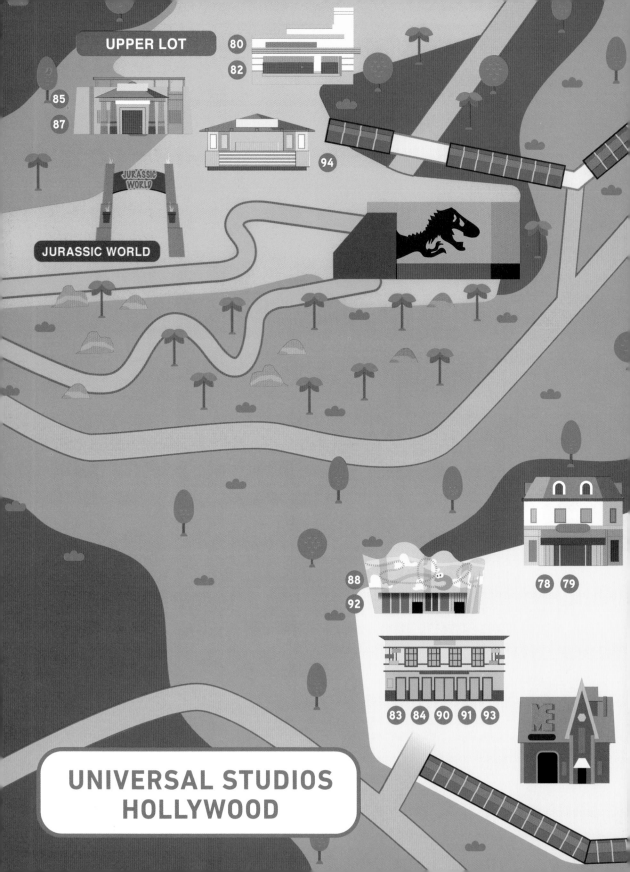

UPPER LOT

80

82

85

87

94

JURASSIC WORLD

JURASSIC WORLD

78 79

88

92

83 84 90 91 93

UNIVERSAL STUDIOS
HOLLYWOOD

KRUSTYLAND

95

86

THE WIZARDING WORLD
OF HARRY POTTER

81

89

LOWER LOT

STANDARD US/METRIC MEASUREMENT CONVERSIONS

VOLUME CONVERSIONS	
US Volume Measure	**Metric Equivalent**
⅛ teaspoon	0.5 milliliter
¼ teaspoon	1 milliliter
½ teaspoon	2 milliliters
1 teaspoon	5 milliliters
½ tablespoon	7 milliliters
1 tablespoon (3 teaspoons)	15 milliliters
2 tablespoons (1 fluid ounce)	30 milliliters
¼ cup (4 tablespoons)	60 milliliters
⅓ cup	90 milliliters
½ cup (4 fluid ounces)	125 milliliters
⅔ cup	160 milliliters
¾ cup (6 fluid ounces)	180 milliliters
1 cup (16 tablespoons)	250 milliliters
1 pint (2 cups)	500 milliliters
1 quart (4 cups)	1 liter (about)

WEIGHT CONVERSIONS

US Weight Measure	Metric Equivalent
½ ounce	15 grams
1 ounce	30 grams
2 ounces	60 grams
3 ounces	85 grams
¼ pound (4 ounces)	115 grams
½ pound (8 ounces)	225 grams
¾ pound (12 ounces)	340 grams
1 pound (16 ounces)	454 grams

OVEN TEMPERATURE CONVERSIONS

Degrees Fahrenheit	Degrees Celsius
200 degrees F	95 degrees C
250 degrees F	120 degrees C
275 degrees F	135 degrees C
300 degrees F	150 degrees C
325 degrees F	160 degrees C
350 degrees F	180 degrees C
375 degrees F	190 degrees C
400 degrees F	205 degrees C
425 degrees F	220 degrees C
450 degrees F	230 degrees C

BAKING PAN SIZES

American	Metric
8 × 1½ inch round baking pan	20 × 4 cm cake tin
9 × 1½ inch round baking pan	23 × 3.5 cm cake tin
11 × 7 × 1½ inch baking pan	28 × 18 × 4 cm baking tin
13 × 9 × 2 inch baking pan	30 × 20 × 5 cm baking tin
2 quart rectangular baking dish	30 × 20 × 3 cm baking tin
15 × 10 × 2 inch baking pan	30 × 25 × 2 cm baking tin (Swiss roll tin)
9 inch pie plate	22 × 4 or 23 × 4 cm pie plate
7 or 8 inch springform pan	18 or 20 cm springform or loose bottom cake tin
9 × 5 × 3 inch loaf pan	23 × 13 × 7 cm or 2 lb narrow loaf or pâté tin
1½ quart casserole	1.5 liter casserole
2 quart casserole	2 liter casserole

GENERAL INDEX

INDEX OF RECIPES
Organized by Intellectual Property (IP)

Note: The following intellectual properties and recipes are featured in the order in which they appear in the book (not alphabetically).

ABOUT THE AUTHOR

Author photo by Valerie Salin

ASHLEY CRAFT has already published three books about the Disney Parks and is excited to finally share her other love with the world: Universal! Many of the Universal franchises have been pivotal in her life, especially the Harry Potter books and films. Ever a loyal Hufflepuff, she can often be found wearing a full robe getup and wielding a wand on any random day of the week. Her first book, *The Unofficial Disney Parks Cookbook*, became an instant bestseller. She lives in Minnesota with her husband, Danny; children, Elliot, Hazel, and Clifford; and kitties, Figaro and Strider. Add her on *Instagram* @unofficialtastetester.

Turn Your
Favorite Cartoon Food
Into REALITY!

THE
UNOFFICIAL
SIMPSONS
COOKBOOK

From Krusty Burgers to
Marge's Pretzels, Famous Recipes from
Your Favorite Cartoon Family

LAUREL RANDOLPH
Foreword by Bill Oakley, Former Showrunner of *The Simpsons*

This book is unofficial and unauthorized. It has not been authorized, approved, licensed, or endorsed by
Twentieth Century Fox Film Corporation, its writers or producers, or any of its licensees.

Pick Up or Download Your Copy Today!

adamsmedia
An Imprint of Simon & Schuster
A Paramount Company